Tactics of Success:

Cover illustration: Des Walker, a defender of
true international quality, stays tactically
close to Gary Lineker, a striker of world
class. Walker can be seen to change his
defensive tactics to best handle the
individual he is marking. (Colorsport/
Andrew Cowie)

▼ The culmination of a swift attack from a goalkeeper's punt. Keith Houchen equalises for Coventry in their 1987 Cup Final triumph over Tottenham Hotspur with a diving header to reach Bennett's cross which has curled between Ray Clemence and his defenders. (Sport & General)

Tactics of Success

Soccer

Nic Paul

**Foreword by
Glenn Hoddle**
Former England International,
Manager of Swindon Town F.C.

WARD LOCK

To George Saunders
Teacher, Coach and Friend

© Ward Lock, 1992

First published in Great Britain in 1992
by
Ward Lock
An Imprint of Cassell
Villiers House, 41/47 Strand,
London WC2N 5JE

British Library Cataloguing-in-Publication Data:
a catalogue record for this book is available from the
British Library

ISBN 0-7063-7089-9

Illustrations by Cilla Eurich.

Designed and edited by DAG Publications Ltd.
Designed by David Gibbons; typeset by
Typesetters (Birmingham) Ltd, Warley, West Midlands;
printed and bound in Great Britain by Clays Ltd,
Bungay, Suffolk.

Contents

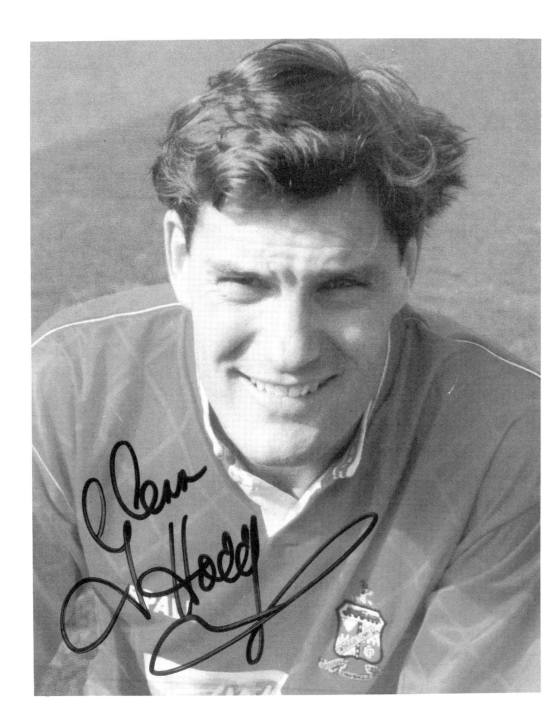

Foreword

by Glenn Hoddle, former England international,
Manager of Swindon Town F.C.

You can enjoy playing and watching soccer without appreciating the tactics of the game, but you will become a better player and a more informed spectator if you are prepared to increase your knowledge of the strategies which make the game so special.

We all get excited when we score great goals or jump from our seats when an attacking movement ends with a fine save or a hard shot on goal. The ball is not saved or cleared, nor does it reach the position where an attempt on goal can be made, without the players involved carrying out the *tactics of success*. If they can employ the right tactics at the right time, or prevent their opponents from doing so, then they will stand a good chance of victory.

In this book you will learn of many of the basic tactics which make up this great game and will read of examples of them being performed by quality players. We all learn our skills from others so I hope you will find that this volume will help you understand and use the *tactics of success*.

Introduction

Even if two teams are hopelessly mis-matched, tactics are still an important part of soccer; and when, as is most often the case, the sides are of similar standard, then tactical supremacy is the most likely route to success. Indeed, a team of inferior individual ability can get the better of their opponents by greater strategic awareness.

The tactics which can be employed in this most popular of international team ball games are endless. The only danger in studying them is that it can nullify natural flair, or make what is essentially a practical game too theoretical. This is certainly the case when a coach or player has a favourite ruse which he seeks to employ too often or where a plan is so technically complex it flounders in the midst of a live match.

In this book we try to avoid complicated theory by demonstrating the tactic in action, achieving success; we replace the chalkboard or table-top with graphics showing the example as it was played. In addition to

benefitting players and coaches, it is hoped the non-playing spectator will be able to watch with more appreciation of the tactical schemes by studying the following pages.

We have sought to avoid the most elaborate tricks and the moves which require outstanding levels of skill – most of them are an amalgam of simpler moves or the province of single players on the ball.

At any age a greater appreciation of the tactical side of soccer will increase enjoyment of it. The author recalls an average youngster who became a very fine 'midfield general' from the moment he was introduced to, and became able to perform, useful running 'off the ball', as opposed to chasing it wherever it went.

The successful team, at any level, is the one that can employ the tactics which suits its own players. To be able to make this decision requires the knowledge of all the soccer *tactics of success*.

▲ To lead your country's attack in a World Cup competition and emerge as the !eading goalscorer is surely a demonstration of quality. Paolo Rossi enjoyed a purple patch in the 1974 and 1978 World Cups when his goals won Italy many games. (Colorsport)

The Long Clearance

● The Tactic

The long punt by the keeper has the obvious benefit of putting the ball in the opponent's half, but it is a vague, unrefined means of doing so unless it is properly exploited by the attacking and midfield players. If a worthwhile attempt to win the ball is not made by the attacking side, then it is simply a means of giving possession back to the opposition.

The kick has to be aimed where the taller players want it, so that their attempt to head it to a colleague has the best chance of success. Ideally the player making the challenge should be surrounded by a 'square' of others from the attacking team, at 10–15 yards distance, so that whatever header he can achieve, a glancing header forward – a very potent attacking move – or back to a supporting player, he has a chance of finding one of his own team.

● Learning the Tactic

① Central attacking players should learn to 'read' their keeper's kicks (e.g., a punt travels with a different trajectory to a drop kick) and should practise the various headers in conjunction with their attacking and midfield team-mates so they can gauge how the ball is likely to come to them.

② As the player jumping to meet the kick is always likely to be closely marked, in training he should always be challenged by a 'defender'.

③ Many attacking moves can be made if clean possession is gained from this situation, and these options should be practised. For example, if a header down to a supporting midfielder is quickly released forward, the consequent rapid change of direction can catch opponents out.

● The Tactic in Use

① This most common of moves is often ignored on the training ground with the result that possession is all too often unnecessarily sacrificed in a game. Used effectively it gains good advantage quickly.

② Ideally, attackers should be rotated in the role of jumper, and all players in this area of the field should be aware of each function they may have to perform.

③ Wind, ground conditions and the height of the opposition all influence how the goalkeeping punt or long defensive clearance is used, but it should be switched with throw-outs and shorter kicks to retain diversity in attacking tactics.

● The Long Clearance Coventry v. Tottenham Hotspur 1987

Cyrille Regis, a typically tall and robust English centre forward, makes an ideal target for goalkeeper Ogrizovic's kick, but the value of his header will be lost if other forwards are

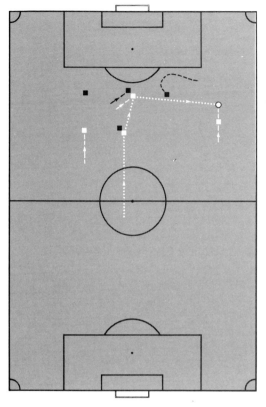
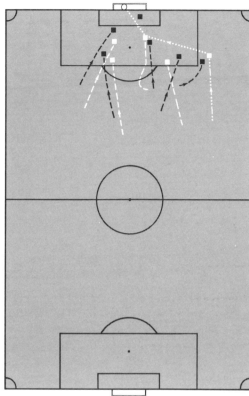

■ Tottenham Hotspur
□ Coventry

not ready to 'feed' off it. Often these headers to clearances can keep the ball moving forward at pace, enabling supporting players to chase the consequent through ball. Here, under challenge, Regis manages to move the ball forward but without pace. Houchen controls the ball but is still closely marked. His pass to Bennett on the right wing is made possible by that player having remained in space and free from defensive markers; the move can therefore progress forward to create one of the finest Cup Final goals.

With Regis now supporting Houchen with a run into the penalty area, Bennett has targets to aim for. There is no attacker at the far post, so his choice is a mid-length, mid-height cross at pace, swinging away from goal between the goalkeeper and the defenders. The cross is played well in front of Regis and Houchen but is curling back towards them; it still demands a lunging volley or diving header to reach it. Houchen launches himself forward to head the ball wide of the stranded keeper. From the punted clearance to hitting the back of the Spurs net, the ball has been in play for 11 seconds.

11

The Cross to the Far Post

● The Tactic

The traditional centre to the goalmouth was aimed at a tall centre forward who met the ball with his head and powered it goalwards. In the more tactically aware modern game, there are differing executions for the same type of cross and one of the most potent is that which sees the deep cross headed back across goal, changing the direction of attack and wrong footing the defence.

Invariably, the forward players in today's game will seek to hunt in pairs for the high cross. One will run to the near post, even if a high centre is expected, both to draw defenders from his team-mate and be ready to 'feed-off' any ball headed wide of goal. The top quality strikers will score a high proportion of their goals from close-in when high crosses go uncleared or are headed on to them.

● Learning the Tactic

① A striking partnership – most successful teams have boasted two quality goalscorers – must build up an understanding of who will take up which positions for such crosses. They will take into consideration height, heading ability and whether either of them favours the right or left foot.

② As ever, much of the training for this tactic should take place against 'de-fenders' so as to recreate a match situation.

③ The player who moves to the near post must have turned and be balanced, ready to attack the ball, by the time his partner is jumping.

● The Tactic in Use

① The perfect header back across goal will be directed downwards to the attacking partner for him to volley or half-volley into goal but often the pass will be at head height or wide of the player, who must be ready to adjust.

② The wide player centring the ball, particularly if he crosses from inside the penalty area, should ensure he runs off the pitch after playing the ball or regains an on-side position as he may be deemed to be interfering with play and offside if he remains near the goal line.

● The Cross to the Far Post: West Germany v. Italy 1970

West Germany reached the 1970 World Cup Final with two of the finest small strikers of the postwar era – Uwe Seeler and Gerd Muller. Seeler, in particular, was an excellent header of the ball and in this example, which levelled the scores at 3–3, he moves to the far

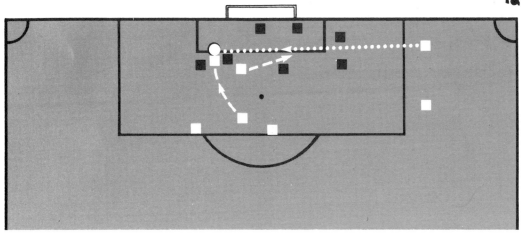

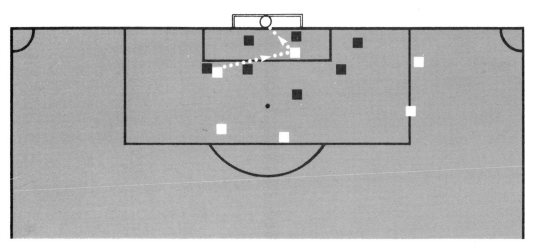

■ Italy
□ West Germany

post for the deep right wing cross whilst his partner, initially better placed for the centre, knows his role is to be ready for any knock down from Seeler.

Despite the attentions of two Italian defenders, Seeler directs the centre back across goal, almost on the same line by which it arrived. Muller is ready to react and does so before goalkeeper and defence by heading the ball home from close range.

It is interesting to note that the Germans had two unmarked men on the edge of the area. High crosses, unless claimed by the keeper, are difficult to clear with distance so the attacking team seems to have catered for every eventuality from this move.

The Cross to the Near Post

● The Tactic

Like so many of the tactics of success, the near post shot or header calls for anticipation as well as basic ability. At the far post the ball is redirected forward but at the near post it has to be glanced at 90 degrees or more, hence the striker must reach the ball ahead of his marker in order to leave the necessary angle open.

Whether or not a soccer team has wide players capable of crossing with such accuracy that they can deliver the near post cross on demand, it should endeavour to get strikers at both near and far posts, to cover all types of centre. Though the deeper player can jump behind a defender and still head the ball goalward, the near post man will usually find it necessary to be in front of his marker, if only by inches, should the ball come to his position.

● Learning the Tactic

① Working as a pair or solo, strikers should train to 'read' a centre as it is played, trying to delay their run to the ball until they can assess its direction and pace.

② Directing a header to the side or behind you takes considerable heading control and timing. Similarly, glancing the ball played to feet, or hooking it towards goal, takes a special skill which should be practised with a variety of crosses from both sides.

③ Wide attacking players should learn to vary their centres and train to look up before crossing to see how and where they should deliver the ball. The near post cross usually needs to be struck faster and lower.

● The Tactic in Use

① The driven cross to the near post is difficult to defend against if the opposition forwards anticipate it well. The defender is often left the sole option of trying to intercept the resulting shot or header.

② The defending goalkeeper finds it less easy to assess the angle the ball will arrive at when it is glanced by head or foot.

③ Attacking players behind their near post colleague must be ready to react to the shorter cross which is headed on or shot across goal.

④ In an attacking pairing it is best for the taller player to concentrate on far post moves, leaving the shorter player to become the near post specialist.

● *The Cross to the Near Post:* Ⓐ
Chelsea v. Leeds United 1970

Two Chelsea defenders are marking centre-forward Jones at the far post as Giles manoeuvres on the left wing. At the near post, Bremner has come through from midfield and it is he who Giles picks out with a low, firm cross which Bremner flicks on across goal. Jones has read the path of the ball better than his markers or the keeper and is able to side foot the ball home from close in.

● *The Cross to the Near Post:* Ⓑ
Manchester United v. Benfica 1968

In this outstanding European final, the Portuguese are finally beaten by a solo goal from George Best, a Brian Kidd header and this near post goal from Bobby Charlton. Albeit deep in extra time, Charlton still finds the energy to not only make a run into the penalty area but then show the alertness to dart to the near post to meet the low, driven cross and flick it right-footed into the net. The defenders have to cut out the cross or reach it before Charlton and do neither, but the United player still has to direct the ball with great accuracy at a target which is narrow and guarded.

A
■ Chelsea
□ Leeds United

B
■ Manchester United
□ Benfica

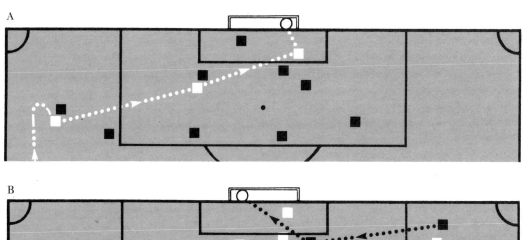

A

B

The Outswinging Cross

● The Tactic

For an attacking team whose forwards are tall or good headers of the ball, the outswinging cross from wide is a crucial element of its game. Properly delivered from a wide position it will have the defenders relying on their goalkeeper to come to collect the ball or having to attempt a clearing header themselves when in retreat or under pressure. If the centre swings away from the goal towards the penalty spot then both keeper and defenders will find it more difficult to decide on their responsibilities, whilst the attacking players will be able to better time their runs and get good contact on the ball.

● Learning the Tactic

① Wide players should practise the angle of cross required from various wing positions. If played from close to the goal line, the outswinging arc required to beat the goalkeeper will take the ball to the penalty spot or beyond, whilst crossing from further back will need the ball to start in the direction of the goalkeeper but swing away from the goal area.

② Central attackers should train to judge their best position dependent on the spot from which the cross is made.

③ The angle of delivery and the attacker's run must meet at a suitable strike point. The pace at which the cross is made will determine when and where the attacker's run is begun.

● The Tactic in Use

① The high outswinging cross should still be played with maximum pace to give the best advantage to the central attackers.

② The extent the cross is used will depend on the height and heading ability of the attacking team and the opposing defence, and the confidence of the defending keeper.

③ The effective outswinging cross is difficult to clear with length and so offers the attacking side the chance of a secondary strike.

● The Outswinging Cross: Italy v. Brazil 1982

Few national sides have better demonstrated the accurate ground pass over the years than the Brazilians, but here it is the Italians who gain advantage by changing the course of their attack with a firm crossfield pass. This new direction and good running off the ball by the Italian forwards causes the Brazilian defence to lose shape and become susceptible to the outswinging cross. Whilst three Brazilian defenders move to counter the new line of advance, Paolo Rossi stays wide on the right. His attacking colleague moves from the inside-left channel to a central position and at this point the ball-carrier might have been expected to dribble on and shoot from long range. Initially it must seem to the Italian defence that the ball is aimed

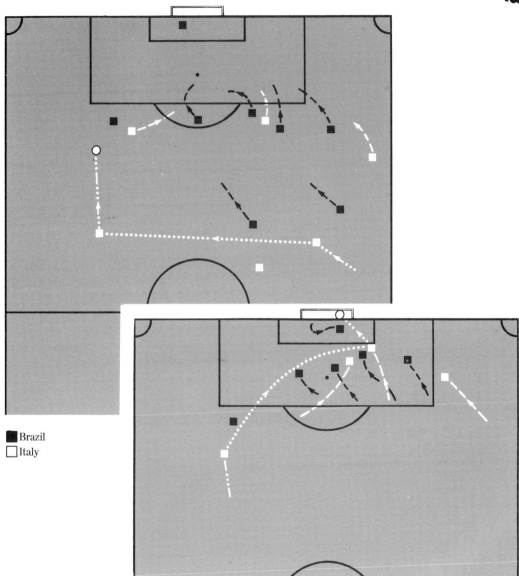

Brazil
Italy

more centrally and certainly the keeper moves to make the save. The outswing, however, takes the ball on a line which is beyond easy reach of the keeper yet behind the retreating defence. Rossi has begun his run as the ball is kicked and, following its trajectory better, needs only to direct his header accurately to be sure of continuing his remarkable scoring record in the 1982 World Cup Finals.

17

▶ Nigel Winterburn, pictured here, and Lee Dixon form a formidable full-back partnership for Arsenal which has perfected the tactic of overlapping in support of the attack. Both players have exceptional stamina and pace, and can cross the ball as well as any specialist winger. (Colorsport)

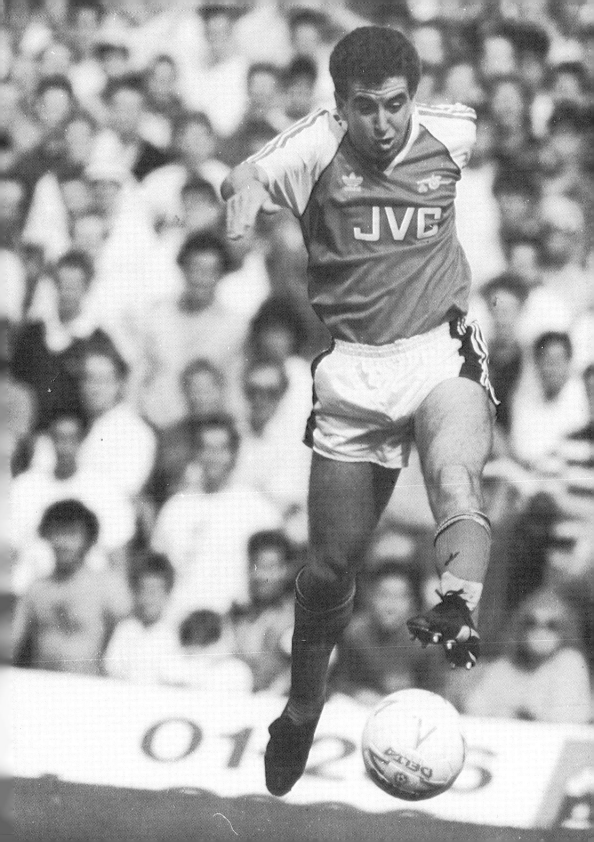

Running with the Ball

● The Tactic

This is the element of attacking play which excites the crowd and panics the opposition, and yet it can be meaningless unless completed by a telling pass or a shot on goal. Defending against an attacker dribbling the ball at pace is difficult and, near or in the penalty area, risky; the first requirement being to get between the ball and your goal so as to cut down the space ahead of the dribbler. Once the attacker has begun his run, however, it is his task to move the ball as far as he can and then make good use of it.

Ill-directed running with the ball can confuse the player's team as much as the opposition and if the dribbler is not aware of colleagues round him, or if he takes his run too far, then the end result may only be exhaustion on his part. Team-mates should endeavour to support the runner as best they can, be ready to accept the pass or close in on any shot he attempts; one of them should also be ready to fill the space he has run from in case the move breaks down.

● Learning the Tactic

① Basic practice in the art of dribbling is fundamental to every training session but this only refines one player's skills. Others should practice running in support, deciding on the prime 'feed off' positions and following in on driven shots at goal.

② In practising dribbling it is essential to perfect the final ball, be it a shot or a pass. All exercises involving running with the ball should ideally involve 'live' defending players or a difficult course of obstacles, and then a final shot or pass.

● The Tactic in Use

① An attacking or midfield player running with the ball attracts defenders to him, thus leaving gaps his colleagues can use provided the dribbler distributes wisely.

② By definition, the runner with the ball is the only one in control of it. Neither team-mates nor opposition can predict his moves – this is the core value of the dribble.

③ Defenders should remember that many sides leave space where the runner has come from so they should be ready to attack that space if they win possession.

● Running with the Ball: Tottenham Hotspur v. F C Porto 1991

Needless to say, a dribble of five yards can be as effective as one of fifty, but here it is the latter which catches the London club out. Having broken down a Spurs attack in their own area, the Portuguese have their defender, Pinto, clear the ball with a short ground pass to substitute, Toze. With fresher legs than the home team's midfielders and receiving the ball clear of markers, Toze turns and runs unchallenged into the Spurs half. Pursuing Spurs players cannot keep pace with the run, leaving four defenders marking two attackers and the approaching Toze.

Up to this point the runner has not been challenged but he knows the Spurs defenders will be drawn towards him. His right winger stays wide to give him a passing option whilst Kostadinov stays on a central run. Here, Toze uses fine close control, switching from right to left foot and back again to weave quickly between two tackles, outpace a third and drive the ball at goal. Keeper Thorstvedt has narrowed the angle but is beaten by the shot which hits the near post only to cannon out to Kostadinov whose run has been made for just such a ricochet.

■ Tottenham Hotspur
□ F.C. Porto

1

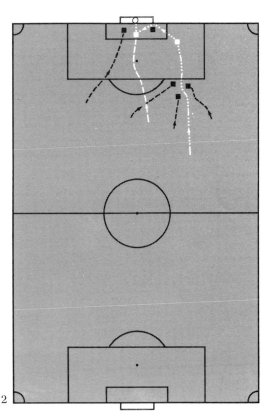

2

Running off the Ball

● *The Tactic*

Since it is the basic rule of all ball games to 'keep the eye on the ball,' it is clear that what happens away from the play is less likely to be noticed. The defending team can often fall into the trap of 'ball-watching' and be caught off-guard by one of their opponents making a move which, though initially not obviously related to the attack being played, can suddenly be used to continue or complete the move.

In making runs which are not directly related to where the ball is, the initial aim is to put yourself in free space where either the opposition is drawn to you and away from others or you can receive a pass and have time to control it without challenge. Coaches refer to this as 'working for each other' and it is the tireless running into space which makes a good side great; Bill Nicholson's fine Spurs team, the Leeds side of the mid-1970s and the Liverpool squads of recent years have been masters of the skill.

● *Learning the Tactic*

① The word 'awareness' occurs several times in this book for it is a pre-requisite of employing successful tactics. In training, coaches must identify routes and spaces players should come to use as second nature.

② The player in possession must learn to look beyond the obvious pass – it is probably obvious to his opponent too! He must watch for the colleague making a run off-the-ball.

③ Unselfish running off-the-ball is tactically valuable even when it is not used in a passing movement. An attacking team in which most players are very mobile is the most difficult to defend against.

● *The Tactic in Use*

① Such running will affect a team's pattern on the field – temporarily at least – and defensive gaps must be covered.

② The pass to a player who has made a sudden move off-the-ball may surprise the rest of his team as much as the opponents and they must be ready to react the quickest.

③ Making space can involve a run of five yards or fifty.

● *Running off the ball: Derby County v. Liverpool 1979*

Combining two dramatic changes of direction and an inspired run off-the-ball, Liverpool produce a classic goal.

Ray Kennedy is inside his own half when his team-mate nearby changes the course of play with a long pass to McDermott on the right wing. The home side no doubt expect Liverpool to gradually build an attack from this new position but Kennedy, now ignored by those watching the ball, has suddenly sprinted forward towards the Derby penalty area.

Noticing this run, McDermott wastes no time in drilling a low first-time cross into Kennedy's path and the midfielder, arriving at pace, controls the ball with one deft touch before walking the ball around the perplexed goalkeeper. Had McDermott not noticed Kennedy's run or chosen not to use it, the

Derby defence would have still had to re-form to mark the move.

McDermott himself was a master of 'running off the ball' and Kennedy was just as likely to be the supplier as the receiver in such moves.

■ Liverpool
□ Derby County

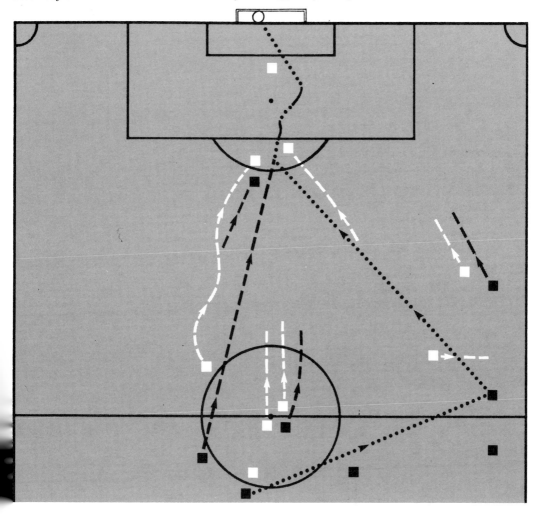

The Overlapping Full Back

● The Tactic

The advantage is usually gained in team sports when one side outnumbers the opposition, especially if this is achieved as a surprise tactic. In rugby this might be by the full-back 'joining the line'; in soccer it is best demonstrated by the full-back overlapping to play as an extra wide attacker and create another offensive option. In both games the move can be used as a decoy and prove equally effective.

Though the winger being marked by the full back in his defensive role is encouraged to track back and reverse their roles in this situation, the surprise element can often ensure the advantage is gained and leave the overlapping player unmarked. This will both cause the defending team to re-form and lose its shape, and provide the attacking team with someone to cross from the flank where before that area might have been vacant or defended man-for-man.

● Learning the Tactic

① The full-back must learn to judge when an overlapping run is required. If he joins too many attacks the surprise element will be lost . . . and so will his energy.

② Full-backs should practise crossing the ball as often as anyone in their team for, if they are going to make the effort to overlap, their distribution at the end of the run must be good enough to reward their initiative.

③ Central attackers must get used to reading their full-backs' centres just as they would those from their wing players.

● The Tactic in Use

① Space for overlapping defenders will often depend on the attacking formation of their own forwards. They should beware of taking their team-mates' space and so reducing their effectiveness rather than improving it by their support.

② The overlapping run often provides the opportunity to add pace to an attack which has ground to a halt.

③ Defenders must be aware of the gap left by a full-back joining an attack. A midfielder may need to stay deep to compensate.

● The Overlapping Full Back: Arsenal v. Tottenham Hotspur 1991

Though not responsible for inventing the tactic, Arsenal might claim to have maximised its use during a period when they enjoyed a regular partnership of Winterburn and Dixon in those positions. Both players are gifted wide players, super fit and in tune with their team-mates. Here are two examples from one game which show the value of the overlapping run as both a decoy run and as a move to keep the attack running.

Ⓐ In the first example Merson is set free by a Smith pass to run at the Tottenham defence. Ahead of him are Bergsson and Fenwick, both seeking to slow his progress by tackle or diversion. Winterburn immediately tracks outside Merson and by doing so attracts the attention of Fenwick who must now ensure he does not leave the overlapping full-back unmarked. This gives Merson sufficient freedom in front of him to attempt a shot on goal.

Ⓑ Later in the same game, Merson receives the ball from a poor Spurs clearance in a similar position. This time he is surrounded by a quartet of defenders and a move forward or inside will be difficult. Instinctively, Winterburn makes his move along the touch-line in support and this time the pass is made, enabling the full-back to run on and make a telling cross into the goalmouth.

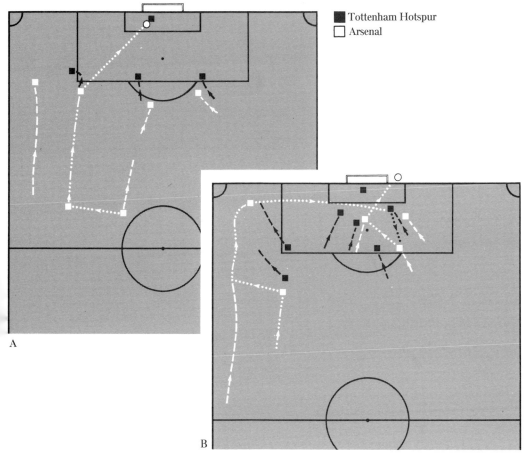

■ Tottenham Hotspur
□ Arsenal

A

B

25

The Diagonal Run

● The Tactic

The forward player attacking on a diagonal run is more difficult to mark than one running straight; he either has to be marked man-for-man or by different defenders as he moves into their space. The midfielder making a through pass to a player running forward has to place his pass directly ahead of the attacker, usually with a lofted pass to avoid defenders; this is more easily read by defenders and the goalkeeper, who can often run out to collect the ball. The diagonal run allows the passer more choice, a lesser likelihood of interception and a wider margin of accuracy.

The midfield player in possession of the ball and seeking to pass to a forward runner can look to play the ball into space wide of the central penalty area. If he selects the right line this can can be made along the ground. He will look to his forwards to begin their runs, even point to where they want the ball delivered, and then select a passing route to that spot. If the run has been effective the forward will have arrived alongside the ball at a position where he can quickly strike for goal or make a useful pass inside.

● Learning the Tactic

① Players at all levels will regularly train for short- and long-distance passes wide of the opposition to their colleagues' feet. They must also practise playing the ball ahead of team-mates making a run.

② Attackers must practise hitting the ball which arrives on a converging line with their diagonal run, from either right or left.

③ Midfielders should train to 'weight' these forward passes so that they arrive conveniently for the run-and-shoot movement of the attacker.

● The Tactic in Use

① The attacker can more easily avoid running offside if his run is diagonal; the defender is drawn to cover the lateral movement and finds it less easy to maintain a straight back line with colleagues.

② Forwards other than the one making the run should take up positions in the central area the runner has left so they can follow in on any shot he makes, or be ready for a centre.

③ The player making the pass should be ready to receive a return ball if he has underhit his pass or the attacker's shooting or crossing routes are cut off.

● The Diagonal Run: Liverpool v. Crystal Palace 1990

Ian Rush has truly mastered this tactic in his play with Liverpool, Juventus and Wales. Here he is Liverpool's lone attacker as Steve McMahon first loses, and then regains, control of the ball in midfield.

Rush is closely marked by one player with another nearby but the latter is caused to concentrate on McMahon's initial forward movement as the breakdown in possession has left the Crystal Palace right-back out of position. McMahon and Rush both see the vacant area where that defender would have been; Rush begins his diagonal run in that direction and McMahon delivers the ball along the ground into the space.

Years of practice and the accumulated skill of both players see that the ball and the centre forward arrive simultaneously a few yards inside the area. Rush is able to beat the attempt at a covering tackle and the goal-keeper's dive by a quick, low shot into the far corner of the net.

■ Crystal Palace
☐ Liverpool

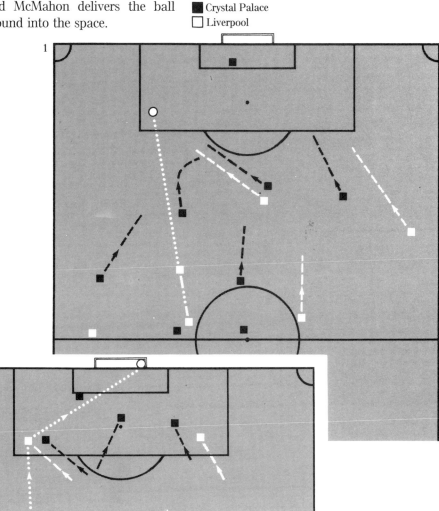

The Through Ball

● The Tactic

Interweaved with the attacking moves of *The Target Man* and *The Diagonal Run*, and the defensive tactics of *The Offside Trap* and *The Keeper as a Defender*, the through ball represents one of the most pleasing soccer tactics to play well, and to watch. The quality midfielders and defenders from the past often achieved their fame by their perceptive passes from centre field, passes which would unlock determined defences and provide great scoring opportunities for their forwards.

If, today, the long pass seems more often to be a hopeful ball with little precision it is probably because of the fact that teams like to get the ball forward faster, rather than the accurate through ball not being used. It has to be remembered that the success of a through ball depends as much on the running and positioning of the forwards as it does on the precision of the passer; perhaps the modern front runners do not have the inventive running of their predecessors.

● Learning the Tactic

① As it is very useful for a forward to build an understanding with one particular midfield colleague, as well as the rest of the team, this move can be trained for as a pair. It is good to put obstacles between the passer and receiver to induce precision – this can be goalposts, other players or freestanding posts.

② The forward must try to make his run so that the pass can be made to his preferred position – the right or left foot, ahead of him or straight to his feet – and colleagues should tolerate and remember these preferences.

③ The decision to play the through ball should never be delayed. The forward will hopefully stimulate the pass by his running or signal and a delay could put that forward offside before the ball is played.

● The Tactic in Use

① The modern game gets compressed in the middle of the pitch, leaving more space behind the defence into which a through ball can be played.

② Though played over a distance, the through ball is still a surprise tactic which can catch a good defence unawares.

③ Pitch conditions have to be borne in mind. A muddy surface can see the ball slow down on first bounce whereas a hard ground topped with wet grass will see the ball skid through, and perhaps make the through ball an unwise tactic.

● The Through Ball: Arsenal v. Tottenham Hotspur 1991

From an Arsenal throw-in just inside their half, Anders Limpar receives the ball and looks to play it forward; this is the signal for Campbell to make his move. The striker, closely marked, begins to peel away to his left into a gap between his marker Bergsson and left-back, van den Hauwe. Seeing this, Limpar curls a right-footed 50 yard pass around Bergsson and into the path of Campbell. As van den Hauwe closes in to challenge, the Arsenal forward pulls the ball behind him and fires a shot across Thorstvedt and into the goal.

This move required Campbell to realise where there was space and appreciate that Limpar's skill could put the ball there. He needed his forward colleague, Smith, to keep Mabbutt occupied. The Swede's through ball needed Campbell's initial move to be followed by pace, control and a good finish to make it the successful tactical move.

■ Tottenham Hotspur
□ Arsenal

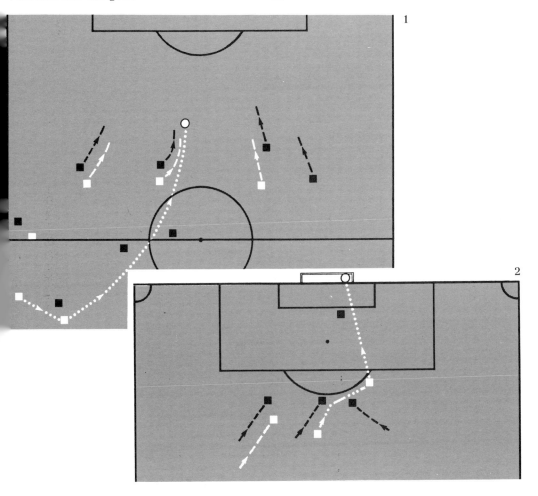

The Wall Pass

● The Tactic

The 'Wall Pass' can be useful in any part of the pitch, to ease the ball quickly out of defence or to make a swift move into the penalty area; in its many guises it is used hundreds of times in a match. Its effectiveness depends on the dual necessities of skill and teamwork – properly deployed it is a most valuable tactic.

The skill factor is on the part of the first player to make the initial pass accurate and then move into a space where the return ball can be played; the second player – the 'wall' – must be able to deliver his pass where his team-mate wants it and at the pace and angle which enables the move to continue. The teamwork element comes not only from the understanding required to execute the move but also the readiness of players to work for colleagues.

● Learning the Tactic

① One of the few 'team' tactics which can be learned 'solo'. The accuracy of the first pass and the run into space can be practised by a single player . . . and a wall!

② The tactic is a regular feature in training but can get monotonous and predictable unless played against determined 'markers' or amidst static obstacles.

③ As it is not always possible to use ground passes, the move should be practised with balls passed at chest and head height.

● The Tactic in Use

① The use of the tactic is dictated by the player making the first pass; he must indicate by his movement that he is expecting the return ball, or is prepared for his run to act as a 'dummy' to the opposition.

② Played at pace, the wall pass is difficult to defend against but used casually or predictably it can simply take the running player out of position.

③ In attack the move is particularly useful against a straight defensive line looking to play the offside trap.

④ The tactic is a means of playing the ball out of defence on the ground and retaining possession but, here, a failure to control the move can prove very costly.

● The Wall Pass: Ⓐ Poland v. England 1991

From a Polish goal kick, Mabbutt's strong headed clearance sends the ball back to Lineker midway inside the home team's half. He quickly passes the ball to Rocastle supporting on the right wing, who, after checking various options – including the overlapping full-back, Dixon, turns inside to play a 35 yard pass to Lineker on the edge of the 'D'. With the two attacking team-mates behind him marked by three defenders, Lineker rightly chooses to play the 'wall' pass' with Rocastle, as the latter invites the return ball by his run into the box.

The perfectly weighted pass puts Rocastle clear for a split second before the goalkeeper and two defenders close on him. His cross from the edge of the goal area is blocked by another Polish defender and the ball flies away for a corner.

The Wall Pass: ⑧ Queen's Park Rangers v. Liverpool 1975

Two ground passes take the ball from Ranger's penalty area to Bowles on the halfway line. His audacious back heel pass sends Gerry Francis into the Liverpool half at pace where his 'wall pass' to Givens is returned accurately as the England captain races clear to hit a firm cross shot past the onrushing Clemence.

This is a fast attacking move involving the delicate skill of Stan Bowles and a perfect example of the wall pass.

A
■ Poland
□ England

B
■ Liverpool
□ Queen's Park Rangers

A

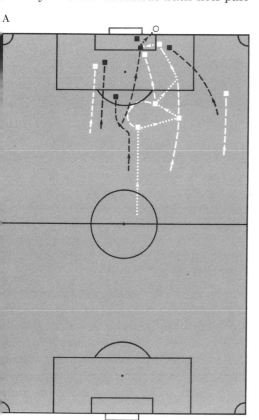

B

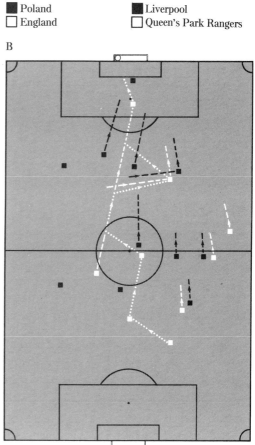

The Target Man

● *The Tactic*

Today's game is played at such a pace, with ten players often required to defend their goal, that the long or sudden clearance to the lone forward can leave him without close supporting team-mates or, at best, with very few colleagues available to pass to. The forward who can keep possession in such circumstances, either by holding the ball or finding another player, is a valuable asset.

All forward players will be put in this position at various times during the game; the star players will have many schemes and tricks for retaining possession and be able to adapt their play depending on how the ball is played to them.

● *Learning the Tactic*

① The pass forward should be accurate. To ask a player to cross the field time after time, usually in a lost cause, serves no purpose. Defenders should practise the long clearance and the through ball in the style of target practice – until they can 'hit' the 'bull'.

② The target man must practise the requisite skills for balls arriving from a distance at various speeds and heights. Close control is physically tiring; stamina is necessary to fulfill this role throughout a game.

③ The target man should always endeavour to maintain the momentum of the attack-ing movement by releasing an accurate pass in front of a team-mate on the move or to one in space.

● *The Tactic in Use*

① The hasty, ill-directed long pass or clearance is simply an easy way of giving possession back to the opposition.

② When the long ball is played to a target man, team-mates must move quickly to get in support of him.

③ If the target man gains possession but can only lay the ball backwards, this has still retained possession and is preferable to the attack breaking up because of an over-ambitious pass.

● *The Target Man: Norwich v. West Ham 1991*

Two moves from this game show the 'target man' in play from passes from midfield rather than hurried clearances.

First, Potts – from just inside the Norwich half – picks out Mike Small as his target man. The ball arrives at head height and though Small does have the support of other forwards they are not close, and are outnumbered. He can only be sure of the support coming from midfield because Slater's move into the area is behind him, out of view.

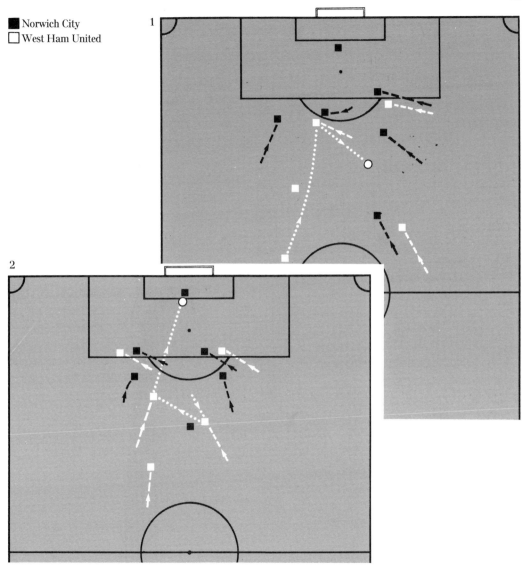

■ Norwich City
□ West Ham United

Small's careful header is backwards to Bishop who plays a first time ball to McAvennie, less well marked. The Scot takes one step forward to get the ball fully controlled and then fires in a shot from 25 yards which the Norwich keeper saves.

Secondly (not illustrated), McAvennie – the smaller of the two strikers – glanced a long pass into the path of Small and a Norwich defender. From the ensuing challenge, Small got control and equalised for the London club.

The Chip Shot

● The Tactic

There can be no more devastating attempt on goal than the chip shot . . . when it works! When it fails – flying high over the bar or dropping tamely into the keeper's hands – hoots of derision will rise from the smallest of crowds!

The chip shot is a rarity if only because the majority mid- and long-range attempts on goal are struck forcefully or with swerve, but, to the goalkeeper moving out to narrow the angle or simply losing position, the ball accurately lofted over him is the perfect attacking tactic as it takes the main defender of the goal out of the game. In junior or lower grade football, teams may encounter a keeper who is especially susceptible to the high shot.

The skill, and alertness, required to deliver an accurate chip, or lofted, shot – we deal with both here – may be inborn but players can still train to establish the prime opportunities for its use and then practise playing it.

● Learning the Tactic

① In practising for the accuracy required, players should place a high (9ft) barrier, or a 'wall' of players, between the outfield and the target goal so as to attempt to loft the ball over this obstacle but under the crossbar.

② Goalkeepers should offer training opposition by running to dive at forwards' feet or deliberately straying off their line so that the chip shot can be practised in all its varieties.

③ Coaches should call for the lofted shot to be tried during practice matches so as to teach outfield players to be aware of its potential use. All players should practise this shot; each will encounter opportunities to use it.

● The Tactic in Use

① Forwards should watch the opposing goalkeeper to detect any tendency to leave his line too often.

② The chipped shot will take longer to reach its target so other attackers should watch for it to be played and be ready to follow up in case pace needs to be added to it.

③ Defenders, likewise, must watch for the lofted shot as they may have time to get back to make a clearance.

● The Chip Shot: Nottingham Forest v. Arsenal 1991

Ⓐ Gemmill wins the ball for the home side inside his own half, passes short and keeps running forward. Clough brings Crosby into play on the right who finds full-back Charles overlapping and takes Winterburn out of the game with a quick pass. Charles runs on to make a cross to Sheringham at the edge of the area who, with his back to goal, sees Gemmill has run on in support of the attack and plays a first time ball into his path.

Keeper Seaman does all he can. He rushes from goal, does not dive too early and gets close to the forward. The Forest player, perhaps expecting Seaman to make a spread-ing dive, lofts the ball over the stranded keeper.

Ⓑ Only minutes later, Merson scores from 18 yards with a delicate chip shot when fed by Rocastle who brings the ball from his own half. The retreating Forest defence mark Campbell and Smith but Merson, overlap-ping Rocastle from midfield, becomes avail-able and, rather than crossing the ball or driving in a shot, chips over Crossley.

■ Arsenal
□ Nottingham Forest

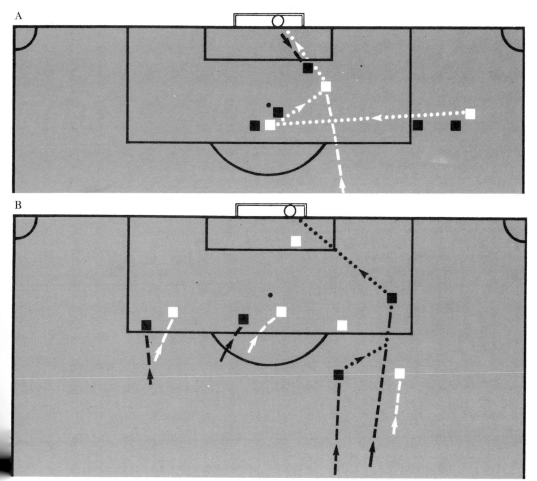

A

B

35

▲ Terry McDermott and Ray Kennedy (background) had a fine understanding in the Liverpool side of the mid-1970s. Both had the ability to play long passes, were fast around the field and were masters at running off the ball. (Colorsport)

▶ The perfect poacher! Denis Law seemed to have a sixth sense when it came to being in the right place at the right time in the goalmouth. His scoring success with all his clubs came from his knowledge that it was his job to get into such situations and use his lightning reactions. (Colorsport)

The Poacher

● The Tactic

How can those who score their goals from inside the goal area, feeding off defensive errors and rebounds, be said to be employing tactics? The answer lies in the fact that 70% of goals are scored from close range and a team can dramatically increase its goal scoring if it has a forward alert enough to get to these positions without being offside.

Most of the great goalscorers have acquired the anticipation and perception which enabled them to pick up loose balls inside the goal area and you will not find the managers and team-mates of Law, Greaves, Muller and Lineker complaining about these aces failing to drive in long range shots. The star strikers can call upon a range of skills to get their close-in attempt on target however the ball comes to them, from a simple tap-in or header to an extravagant overhead kick or a 'turn on a sixpence.'

● Learning the Tactic

① The front players should practise following in on the goal attempts of others. Coaches must call for such runs to be made at every opportunity in training until it becomes second nature to the player.

② These players should train in the six-yard box with passes being made from every direction, pace and height so as to experiment with the many ways of directing the ball goalwards.

③ As the most common miss in front of goal is placing the ball too high, headers and volleys should always be kept down.

● The Tactic in Use

① If the attempt on goal is blocked, parried or hits the goalposts, the attacking side still gains reward if its players are alert to every loose ball.

② The poacher will usually be judged to be interfering with play, and offside, if he is in such a position when the ball is struck back in by a colleague. He must be ready to run back to a deeper position whenever the ball is cleared.

③ A goal scored from one yard counts the same as one hit from thirty!

● The Poacher: Ⓐ England v. Scotland 1967

Denis Law was a prime exponent of this art in the 1960s and 70s. Though he scored fine goals running from deep, he was a master in the crowded goal area.

In this match Law scores a typically opportunistic goal in the first 'old rivals' match after the 1966 World Cup. Law is close to a skirmish on the edge of the England penalty area as the ball breaks clear to a team-mate who strikes for goal. By the time the shot is parried by Banks, Law is on hand to react to the sharp ricochet and flick the free ball into the empty net.

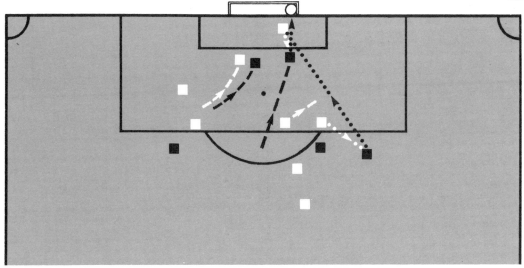

A

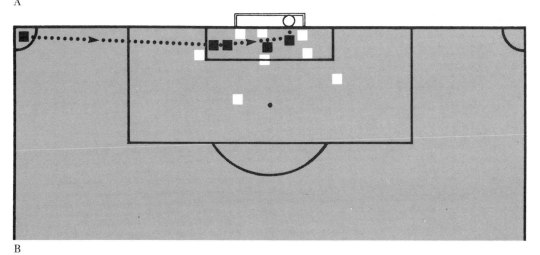

B

A	B
■ Scotland	■ Mexico
☐ England	☐ Belgium

● *The Poacher:* ⑧
Belgium v. Mexico 1986

Hugo Sanchez of Mexico and, adoptively, of Real Madrid, was the scorer of some spec-tacular goals but he was just as happy to score from close in and celebrated with equal exuberance however he scored. Here, a left wing corner is flicked on at the near post and Sanchez does not have to move his feet to head home. The ball arrives at pace, how-ever, and he shows the lightning reactions of the poacher to deflect it goalwards rather than high or wide.

The Direct Free Kick

● *The Tactic*

There are many ways in which the direct free kick can be used, including the variations when a shot at goal is not considered. Here we only look at the attempt on goal and have to immediately recognise that not every soccer player can kick the stationary ball with the power, accuracy or swerve of a Pele, Platini or Barnes.

Even these great stars benefitted from a badly-positioned or disrupted wall and it is here that any football team can improve their chances at direct free kicks around the edges of the penalty area. Once the defending team has formed its 'wall' at ten yards – and, hopefully, the referee will have insisted on that distance – one or two of the attacking team can place themselves in front of it. As the kick is being taken, and the value of someone dummying to take the kick is considerable here, these players can quickly move to the side; defenders have to be concentrating very hard to avoid following this sudden movement which will leave a gap in the barrier they have formed and allow the kicker to have a free line to goal.

● *Learning the Tactic*

① All attacking players must know the strategy which is to be used. By a sign or the call of a letter or number they must know the positions to take up. Each devised movement must be practised extensively so that timing is perfected,

and several such alternatives may be needed.

② Everyone involved in the free kick strategy should have a secondary role if the kick is not successful, i.e. looking for the rebound off the 'wall', following the shot, or be ready for ricochets off the goalkeeper or the posts.

● *The Tactic in Use*

① The strategy chosen when a suitable kick is awarded must be quickly selected and 'called'.

② Though the same movement can be used more than once against the same opposition, it is likely that a dozen or more options will be needed and regularly used.

③ Of direct free kicks taken 18–30 yards from goal, only 1% result in the first shot scoring but a further 6% are converted by secondary moves following up rebounds or poor clearances resulting from the kick.

● *The Direct Free Kick:* Ⓐ *Brazil v. Czechoslovakia 1970*

Few international players have shot more powerfully than Rivelino. He could strike a ball in every fashion, hard and low, high and curving, over ten yards and fifty. It seemed a futility to set a defensive wall against him.

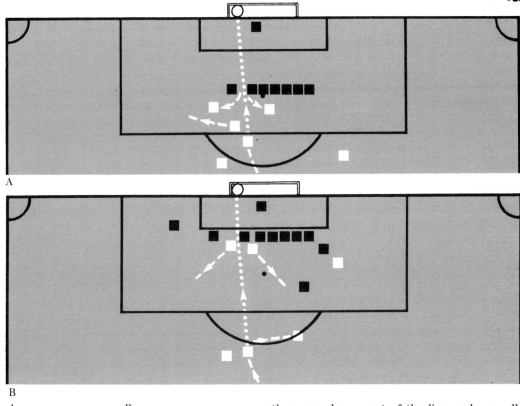

A

B

A		B	
■	Czechoslovakia	■	Manchester United
□	Brazil	□	Tottenham Hotspur

Here the Czech team line up no less than seven players supposedly to force the Brazilian to choose an alternative to the direct shot. The South Americans, however, put two of their own men in front of the wall on the right side.

Four Brazilians are in a position to take the kick and the Czechs cannot be certain it will be Rivelino until he is in his approach. As he reaches the ball, the Brazilians in the wall each dart sideways, in opposite directions; the defenders immediately behind them are drawn out of the line and a small gap is left. Though Rivelino still swerves the ball, the direct path to the goal enables him to hit the ball with greater pace. The goalkeeper barely moves.

● *The Direct Free Kick:* Ⓑ *Tottenham Hotspur v. Manchester United 1973*

Showing that even professionals are prepared to copy, from a similar position Spurs surround the ball, put two players in the wall and achieve the same result when, as Peters runs over the ball, the Spurs players dash from the wall, and Knowles curls home a fine left-footed shot.

The Short Free Kick

● The Tactic

There are so many tactics which can be employed at free kicks. Depending on the position where the kick is being taken, it can be played as a pass deep into the opposition penalty area, to a wide player who can then cross it, as a calming pass back to the keeper, or to a nearby team-mate to retain possession.

It is very often the most attacking move, as well as the safest, to play a free kick short to a team-mate who can progress an attack. This takes awareness on the part of at least two players and, ideally, the whole team. Awareness is a massive asset; you can be certain it will bring easy rewards against many teams.

When a free kick is awarded the option of a short pass, especially made quickly before the opposition defence has re-formed, should always be considered.

● Learning the Tactic

① It is worthwhile for pairs of players, usually one from midfield and one attacker, to devise a tactic for such free kicks which they can use at particular positions without any sign other than a glance at each other.

② The secret, for an attacking team awarded a free kick, is for front and wide players to make moves quickly which will allow the short kick option to be used;

they can always reposition for a longer kick.

③ Every member of the team must train to react quickly to the whistle and assume useful positions in space or begin to make runs.

● The Tactic in Use

① The player initiating a quick free kick must not be hindered by team-mates offering alternative suggestions. If his plans fail a couple of times then more caution may be required.

② By taking such a kick a team is often able to employ a tactic which it has previously found it difficult to create, i.e. space to cross from wide.

③ A short, simple pass to a colleague in space may be valuable in calming players down and allowing them to regroup.

● The Short Free Kick: Leeds United v. Manchester United 1991

Ⓐ Strachan is fouled halfway inside the United half. Rather than allow the opposition time to re-form he looks to Wallace, inviting him to run into space, and only a lunging tackle from Bruce prevents the forward from getting a clear shot on goal.

Ⓑ In a similar situation later, Strachan again side-foots a free-kick into space, to the overlapping Dorigo, and so presents a more positive attacking move than a hopeful ball into the packed area. Dorigo's cross is well delivered but successfully defended.

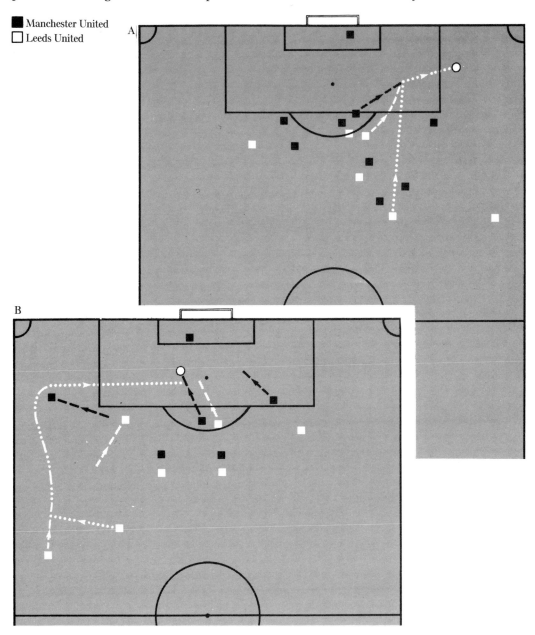

■ Manchester United
□ Leeds United

The Penalty Kick

● The Tactic

Of course, the primary aim with a penalty kick is to make it count, to score. But tactics can, indeed must, be considered even with this straightforward 'shoot-out at 12 yards.'

Since failure to convert a penalty kick is the ultimate depressant to any team spirit, those chosen for the task should not suffer from lack of practice. They should take as many kicks as often as possible, in as different conditions as they can find and against the best possible goalkeepers. They should be able to treat the goal as a dart-board and place their kick precisely where they have chosen; to this end, practice against a wall is entirely sensible.

The player taking the kick must have learnt the rules set out below, understand the best parts of the net to aim for and be ready to change his normal style if presented with more than one opportunity in a match.

● Learning the Tactic

① Look at this chart to see the areas of his goal a diving keeper finds it most difficult to reach, and concentrate your aim there.

② Keep a consistent run-up so that you are sure of being balanced when you reach the ball.

③ Be absolutely sure where you are trying to place the ball, and never change your mind whilst running up.

● The Tactic in Use

① If well placed the hard-hit shot is always more likely to beat the dive, but most players can control the direction of their shot better if they play it with less pace.

② If the shot is beaten out by the keeper the kicker should be ready to score from the rebound. If it rebounds off a post, a team-mate or opponent must touch it before he does.

③ It is sad to see many professionals strike a penalty kick to the centre of the goal and still score because the keeper has dived. Whilst this can be successful, accurate kicks to the bottom and top corners of the net are very seldom fairly stopped.

● The Penalty Kick: Ⓐ Portugal v. England 1966

Eusebio lit the 1966 World Cup competition like a beacon; everything he did had class, including his penalty kicks which he could hit fast or slow, high or low, but always cleanly and decisively. Here he brings his side back into the semi-final against England with a side-footed shot stroked inside Gordon Banks' right-hand post. The accuracy of the kick placed the ball beyond any dive Banks could complete without moving before the ball was played.

● *The Penalty Kick:* Ⓑ *Liverpool v. Leeds United 1974*

To win the Charity Shield match at Wembley, Ian Callaghan strikes his kick firmly to Harvey's right as the goalkeeper moves left. In truth, the kick was not well placed – the Liverpool player slipped as he hit the ball – but it was firm and decisive. Had the keeper delayed his dive a split second longer he may have been able to make a save.

● *The Penalty Kick:* Ⓒ *Sheffield Wednesday v. Leeds United 1992*

John Sheridan hits his penalty hard but neither along the ground nor high enough; Lukic makes a great attempt to stop the ball, palming it onto the inside of his right-hand post. The ball rebounds across the goal but with the keeper on the ground, Sheridan is able to follow up and tap the ball home.

● *The Penalty Kick:* Ⓓ *Notts County v. Manchester United 1992*

Clayton Blackmore, renowned for his power of shot from distance, strikes his penalty with venom. The County keeper guesses correctly and dives quickly but the strength of the shot, combined with its accuracy, sees it fly into the corner.

1	2	2	3	3	2	2	3	3	2	2	1
1 Ⓓ	3 Ⓒ				4	4				3	1
2	Ⓑ 3									3	2
1 Ⓐ	2									2	1

▲ The target area for penalty takers assuming a full dive by the goalkeeper. Once he is committed to the dive then the opposite side of the net is open but for practice sessions players should aim for sectors numbered 1 and 2, noting that mid-height shots are more easily reached by the diving keeper.

45

▲ Rivelino brought power to the established finesse and artistry of Brazil's midfield in the World Cup final stages of 1970 and 1974 His skill at dead ball situations created goalscoring opportunities where they could not exist for other teams. (Colorsport)

▶ A 1959 photo of Bobby Charlton who graced the game through to the 1970s. Apart from the blistering pace of his shots from distance, Charlton had the ability to pass the ball over any distance with great accuracy and, perhaps his greatest asset, play his own starring role whilst bringing the best out of the other top players around him. (Sport & General)

The Corner Kick – 1

● *The Tactic*

The corner kick in amateur football often becomes a hopeful cross into a crowded goalmouth where the attacking team bank on a lucky break giving them a goalscoring chance. Though it takes skill to place a corner kick exactly where colleagues require, even this counts for little if they do not have the tactical awareness to use it.

We particularly consider here corners to be delivered to the goal area, but both the short corner, enabling the centre to be made from a different angle and with a moving ball, and the low driven corner to a team-mate prepared for such a move, can be very effective.

It is so often the support players who become important at corners; for example, those watching for ricochets inside the goal area or those covering the partial clearance.

● *Learning the Tactic*

① Those waiting for the kick must be used to the style of the player taking it so they can time their runs accordingly.

② Attackers not making the first challenge for the cross must try to cover as many of the angles in which the ball might travel when it is first played. One might stay close to the goal-line to tap in any knock down, others might be a few yards in front and behind the jumper and some midfielders must be stationed on the edge of the penalty area.

③ In practising corner kicks, realistic 'opposition' must be used whenever possible.

④ It is, of course, wise to use the natural curl of the ball off the instep to create inswinging and outswinging corners, and to have the corners taken by those who can most accurately play the ball in this manner.

● *The Tactic in Use*

① If tall defenders are used in an attacking role at corners, team-mates must cover their positions.

② It is seldom wise to crowd the area close to goal; it is good to have some of the support players arriving from further out.

● *The Corner Kick – 1: Manchester United v. Derby County 1970*

Any team would benefit from having Bobby Charlton take their corners. The master of the shot from distance had marvellous accuracy as well and his corners fell just where they were supposed to. In this remarkable high scoring draw, Charlton's kicks kept his team in the game.

Ⓐ An inswinging corner from the right to the near post is met by Sadler, whose glancing header is only parried by the keeper. The bouncing ball is hooked into the net by George Best. This style of corner kick is commonly used now, with a tall attacker heading a near-post kick on into the goal-mouth.

Ⓑ From the opposite corner Charlton sends a cross to the middle of the goalmouth. Although Derby outnumber United 9 to 5 in the penalty area, at the point where the ball is delivered only two can make a challenge

■ Manchester United
□ Derby County

for it. It beats both of them and falls to Denis Law who heads wide of the keeper without pressure.

Ⓒ To draw the match Brian Kidd heads home another Charlton corner from the right. The United defender, Ian Ure, draws a defender to the near post so Charlton delivers the ball over this pair to where Kidd can more easily outjump the remaining defenders and send his header beyond the keeper and two other players on the line.

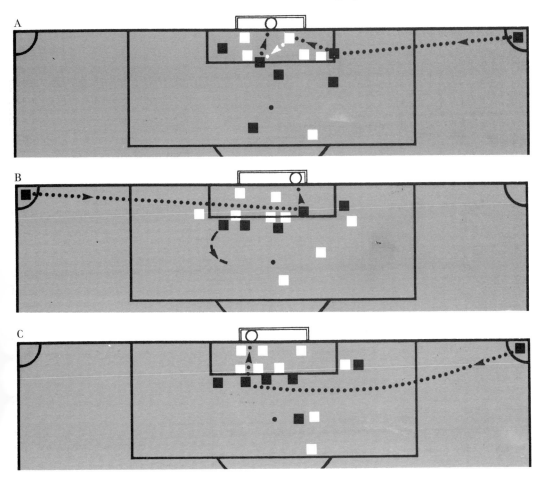

A

B

C

The Corner Kick – 2

● The Tactic

Apart from the kick to the crowded penalty area which, however well delivered, has an element of the imprecise, there are several other means by which the valued advantage of a corner kick can be well used. A side is well advised to have a variety of tactics practised so as to keep the opposition guessing.

The tapped kick to a nearby team-mate can allow the centre to be delayed and then made at a different angle, the near-post corner can be headed on into the centre of the goal area or glanced towards the net, the deep cross can often allow a late runner to get a free header even if it may be from some distance, and the low, driven ball can be a useful option if the attacking side has someone waiting for it.

● Learning the Tactic

① Forwards, and the defenders who may move up for corners, should train as required to be able to use as many options at corners as possible.

② Certain needs remain the same for all corners, i.e. back-up players at the edge of the area for poor clearances, adequate defensive cover if tall defenders have moved forward, etc.

③ Most of the alternatives discussed here involve an initial move for the ball which must be followed up by colleagues feeding off the first play.

● The Tactic in Use

① A team which wins the most corners should win the game but may not unless they are able to make good use of them in a variety of ways.

② Both the near-post header and the efficient use of a driven cross require a high level of skill and should not be attempted unless a team has the players capable of delivering or using them.

③ Using awareness again, a team able to take position for a corner, and play the ball, before the defence is similarly organised, should gain an advantage.

● The Corner Kick: Ⓐ England v. Poland 1991

From a right-wing corner, the closest Polish attacker, marked by the full-back, Pearce, makes a sudden move backwards from the edge of the six-yard box towards the penalty spot, taking the England player with him. At the same time, Kosecki runs forward into the resulting gap. These swift moves take place as the kick is being taken so as to have Kosecki arrive level with the near post as the driven corner reaches that point.

Such has been the pace of the move that he enjoys a free header before Pearce can make the adjustment to cover the new threat. The accurate header dips to the foot of the post but Woods is able to dive and gather the ball.

50

● *The Corner Kick:* ⑧ *Leeds United v. Crystal Palace 1992*

The much-used near-post headed-on corner is used here by Leeds. Their opponents do the right thing by marking the tall Whyte at the front post and correctly guess that is where Strachan will aim his kick. They are outwitted, however, by Speed who runs forward to a position in front of those watching Whyte and is able to head the ball backwards across goal to where Fairclough is able to stab the ball home.

■ Poland
□ England

A

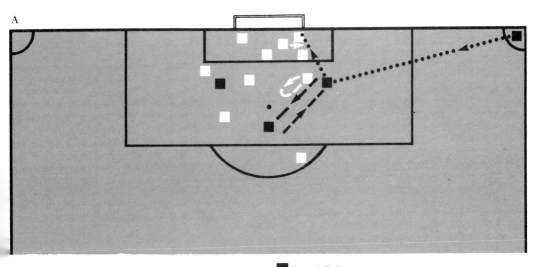

■ Crystal Palace
□ Leeds United

B

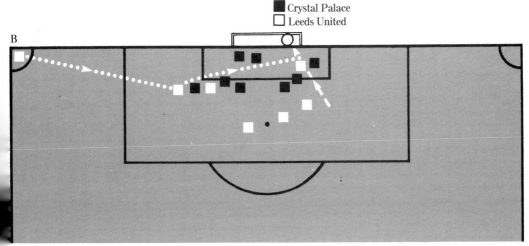

The Throw-In

● The Tactic

Even in the most professional of matches, the throw-in can still be used tactically, be a potent weapon in offensive play and should be practised in its diverse forms. If one team forces the opposition to concede a throw-in, they should be alert enough to avoid giving possession back by virtue of an ineffectual throw.

It is alertness, awareness, which is most important in this aspect of the game. The player making the throw needs to be presented with the maximum number of options and has to rely on his own and team-mates' watchfulness to create these alternatives.

In the last third of the attacking field, the long throw has become increasingly prevalent, even in youth and junior football, but the majority of throws occur where such a tactic cannot be used. There must be constant and constructive movement by the thrower's colleagues and the throw should be able to be made to the place that will allow for it to be played under control and possession retained.

● Learning the Tactic

① Even senior teams can benefit from incorporating the throw-in into their training schedules. This will increase understanding in a match situation.

② Train to take up positions where the thrower and the receiving player both have options available. If the ball is thrown to feet, practise its accurate delivery back to the thrower or a supporting player; if it is delivered to the head, team-mates must be ready for the glancing header on or the defensive header backwards.

③ The long throw-in is a valuable tactic and it is good for each team to have at least one exponent. Those who will be manning the penalty area where such throws land should practise 'feeding off' the subsequent headers.

● The Tactic in Use

① To ensure possession is retained, a defensive throw to a player in space, albeit behind the line of the throw, may be preferable; this throw must be accurate and the recipient clear of markers.

② The throw down the line, even if intercepted by the opposition, can still put opponents under pressure and is the most frequently-used throw.

③ The quick throw, made possible by early and effective running into space by team-mates, can still catch the best defence off-guard and a player regularly making such runs is of great value.

● The Throw-In: Arsenal v. Benfica 1991

Each game will present a multitude of throw-in options and often more than thirty throws

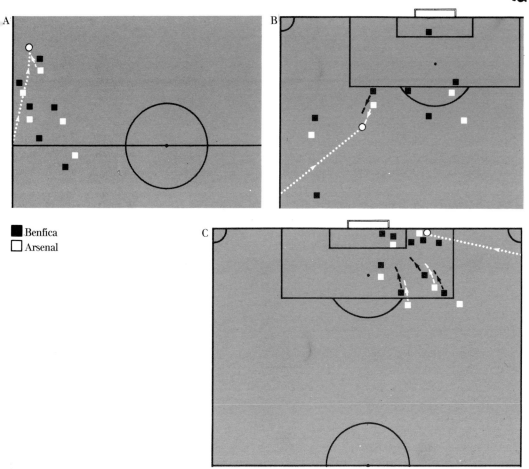

Benfica
Arsenal

These three examples from one game were effective in that they put pressure on the Portuguese side.

Ⓐ Winterburn throws the ball close to the sideline, to one of a quartet of Arsenal players in positions forward of himself. Smith, who jumps to head the ball on to Campbell, has the choice of heading back to two other team-mates so the London club had good chances of retaining possession.

Ⓑ From just inside the opposition half,

Winterburn chooses the option of a quick mid-range throw to Campbell who has briefly moved clear of his marker and so has a better chance of controlling the ball before being challenged.

Ⓒ Here, Dixon fires a high, long throw-in to the Benfica six-yard box. He has waited until his tall jumpers are in the positions they will have practised in training and used in games. Such throw-ins carry the same attacking threat as a near-post corner.

The Swift Attacking Movement

● The Tactic

The efficient use of pace is a worthy asset in most team games. In soccer it is more often demonstrated by one or two members of a side but when employed by several players, taking the ball from defence to attack, it is a joy to spectators and soul-destroying for opponents. In training, a team might practise running the length of the field, exchanging passes, but in a match situation players will find a range of skills will be needed to be used to outwit an alert opposition.

Such a move, when successfully employed, is likely to include close control, one-touch ground passing, clever running off-the-ball and, perhaps, heading and the lofted pass. It might be argued that such a complete footballing move cannot be termed a tactic, and cannot be trained for, but this limits the aims of any group who want to achieve soccer excellence. As can be seen from the example used, the secret lies in stamina and teamwork; the required skills are the basic ones practised for simpler tactics.

● Learning the Tactic

① Teams practising as an 'eleven' will have to invent an opposition with the coach 'calling' for the moves, the sudden changes of direction and the pace a match situation will produce.

② Though there need not be a link man in a swift passing movement, it is advisable that the tactic is centred around the team members who have extra pace and passing skills.

③ It should be understood that a rapid passing movement must not involve so many of the team that it is left without sufficient cover if the move breaks down. Team-mates should train to notice defensive gaps, and fill them.

● The Tactic in Use

① The quickfire attacking movement usually builds from one or two passes, or an inspired example of running off-the-ball, when gaps become apparent and runners are left unmarked.

② The tactic is particularly advantageous against opposition whose defence of the high ball or the long pass is better than ground passing and running.

③ The opportunity to attack from deep and at pace comes more readily late in a game when the opposition may be tiring but, again, over-committment of numbers to the move is still unwise.

● The Swift Attacking Movement: West Ham v. Liverpool 1991

In a remarkably fluid movement covering most of the field, West Ham show their traditional flair, 'letting the ball do the work,' in posing a threat to the Liverpool goal just 12 seconds after taking a throw-in close to their own goal line. Seven players are involved in the move, each playing the ball just once; one of them, Stuart Slater, is closest to the throw-in when it is taken yet finishes up chasing the final pass into the Liverpool area – 80 yards in 12 seconds – receiving and distributing the ball in the middle of his run!

The throw-in is sent beyond Slater to McAvennie who immediately feeds Bishop running clear of defence. His quick pass finds Keen in midfield and he moves the ball onto Slater who has sprinted forward in support. This perfectly-weighted ball enables Slater to pass first-touch to right-back Breaker who has found a great deal of space and is able to run forward into the Liverpool half. Slater, still racing forward, stimulates Breaker into attempting the final pass through the Merseysiders' defence. The ball is well directed and this most impressive attack is only thwarted by the alertness of keeper, Grobbelar, who dashes outside his area to fly-kick clear.

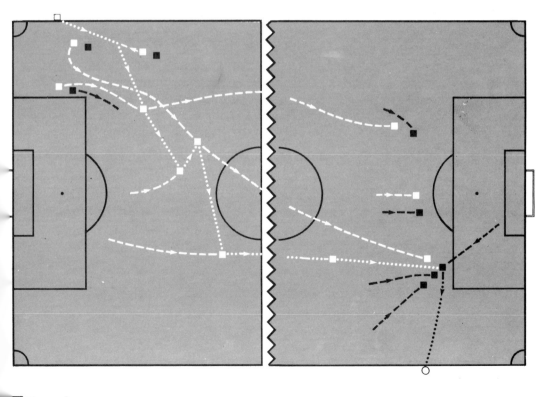

■ Liverpool
□ West Ham United

The Late Attacking Run

● The Tactic

As with the overlapping run of a full-back, the late arrival of a midfielder in and around the penalty area has the immediate benefit of increasing the number of attackers that have to be watched by the defence. If a team has a player who can regularly make such moves, the opposition can even find it necessary to retain an extra defender to cope with these runs if and when they are made.

Joining an attack late offers the player a preferential perspective. He can see gaps his team-mates cannot and can better judge the flight and pace of crosses. As his forwards make runs towards or off the ball, and take marking defenders with them, the late runner can have a telling effect. There have been many international stars whose reputations have grown because of their success with this tactic – Franz Beckenbauer, Martin Peters and Bryan Robson are examples.

● Learning the Tactic

① It is not a God-given sixth sense which persuades a midfielder to make a late run into the penalty box. It is hours of practice with team-mates, experiments in match situations and watching the move successfully used by others which brings the skill required.

② It is often wise for a team to devise specific attacking methods which will utilise the late run, although it will more often be an opportunistic move brought

about by the circumstances of the game.

③ Those crossing the ball, or in possession of it in attacking positions, should train themselves to look for the late runner behind their attacking team-mates.

● The Tactic in Use

① There can be few attacks which cannot benefit from a midfielder making a late run, even if it is to distract defenders, but to rely overmuch on the tactic can reduce its impact and tire the players concerned.

② The tactic is particularly relevant against man-to-man marking, or in countering a massed defence which is concentrating on one or two attackers.

③ The late run deprives the attacking team of one midfield or defending player so compensation should be made by his colleagues in case possession is lost.

● The Late Attacking Run: Ⓐ Arsenal v. Manchester United 1970

The long ball to the edge of the United penalty box is chased and controlled by Radford. With only Kennedy upfield in support, Radford waits until Armstrong joins him on the left wing so that he can pass short and move inside to join Kennedy. Armstrong, however, spots the late run from midfield by George Graham and his accurate pass allows the Scot to send a glancing header inside the far post.

● *The Late Attacking Run:* Ⓑ *Everton v. Liverpool 1977*

A long clearance finds Mackenzie and Pearson as the only Everton forwards in attacking positions. Mackenzie heads to his colleague and runs wide for the return ball but Pearson is tackled and unable to make ground into the penalty area for Mackenzie's cross. The attack is made successful by a determined forward run by midfielder Rioch who arrives just in time to side-foot the ball into the net.

A
■ Arsenal
□ Manchester United

B
■ Everton
□ Liverpool

A

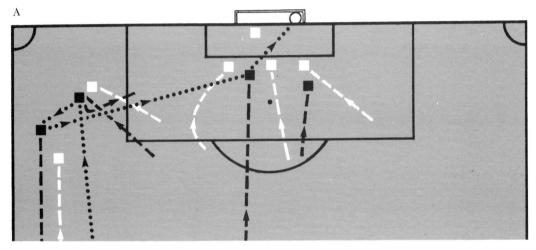

B

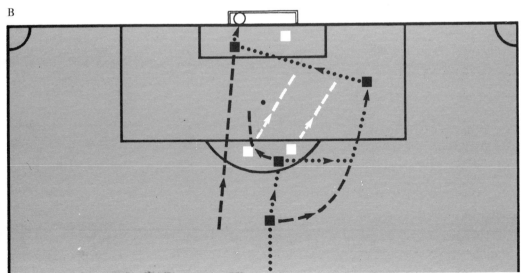

▲ Described by his England manager as "years ahead of his time", Martin Peters was one of the finest exponents of the late attacking run into the penalty area and achieved a higher-than-average scoring record from midfield. (Colorsport)

▲ Bryan Robson's role as a combative, ball-winning midfielder for England and Manchester United has fortunately not hindered his excellent goalscoring performances brought about by the ability to make late runs from deep. Here he is seen in action against West Germany in the 1982 World Cup. (Sport & General)

Changing the Direction of Play

● *The Tactic*

Much of the movement up and down the field during a soccer match is predictable and commonplace. In such circumstances it is the unexpected that can destroy your opponents pattern and cause them to panic. When it is used in mid-move, by an astute change of direction in the play by one or two players, the effect can be dramatic.

It is human nature to be drawn towards the ball, where you expect it to be played and to players running into routine positions. If, without warning, you transfer the ball to a team-mate in space, in a position which does not seem necessary for the opposition to defend, then their attention is distracted, the players within the earlier play area are likely to be forgotten, at least for a moment, and completely new attacking tactics can be deployed.

● *Learning the Tactic*

① In training games, coaches must urge midfield players in particular to consider changing the direction of play, and ensure a team-mate or two stay in position to be used for such purpose.

② By definition, the passes required to change the direction of attack always need to be accurate, usually played over some distance, and must not be predictable.

③ Once the direction of play has been changed the rest of the team must move in support, close or at distance, of the new player in possession.

● *The Tactic in Use*

① The use of this tactic should be more tiring to defend against than to play. A tired opponent is one against whom tactical play becomes even easier.

② The pass which changes the direction is usually to the wide positions and is therefore especially useful against teams with weak full-backs or particularly good central defenders.

③ The area on the pitch from which the long pass has been made suddenly becomes ignored and an immediate switch of play back in that direction can be useful.

● *Changing the Direction of Play:*
Leeds United v. Tottenham Hotspur 1973

Johnny Giles was an effective passer over five or fifty yards and a master of changing the direction of attack by making just one unexpected move.

Jones wins the ball on the centre spot and passes to his striking partner, Clarke. The ball is moved onto Giles close by and both Jones and Clarke move off into the Spurs half. Giles facing the left wing, is expected to retain safe possession by a back pass or one to wide on the left, although he must also be considering a through ball for Jones and Clarke to pursue. Instead, he instantly twists and sends a 40-yard pass to the right wing, behind Bremner, to Lorimer.

The Tottenham team is now turned and their defence has to defend off-the-ball runs from new angles. Lorimer, himself, runs a few yards into the Spurs half before sending a through ball to the fast-running Bremner who has found a new line of attack brought about by Giles' move. The Leeds captain allows the ball to come alongside him before sending a volley wide of the keeper.

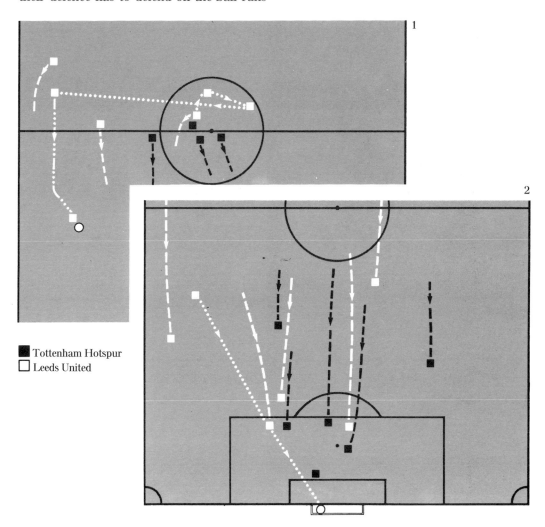

■ Tottenham Hotspur
□ Leeds United

The Defence at Corner Kicks

● The Tactic

The corner kick represents a frequent means by which a defence will be put under extreme pressure and must be ready to apply tactical thinking on how to counter the threat.

A defence must be reactive, but not make panic moves. If their opponents offer a threat at corners because of their height then clearly the players concerned must be marked by the most suitable members of the defending team. They must also, however, never forget the basics of defence in these circumstances: cover the goal-line, especially if the keeper moves out to catch or punch; mark the players on the edge of the area as well as those within it; always have a player forward of the near post to get to the low or mis-hit corner first, and so on.

The defence which has no policy for corners is the one which will be scored against from them most often. Have players specialise in undertaking set duties.

● Learning the Tactic

① A goalkeeper must be as dominant at corner kicks as his ability allows and should train to establish which type of corner he can safely jump for. In a game he should try to be consistent so his players can know when he is likely to leave his line.

② Whether or not the goalkeeper attempts to catch or punch the ball, the goal-line must be defended. One player at each post is traditional and sensible; it will save several goals in a season.

③ A headed clearance may not travel far. Other members of the defending team must be ready to add distance to such clearances and those outside the six-yard box should also mark the late run and secondary strikes of the opponents.

● The Tactic in Use

① The keeper should 'call' if he plans to leave his line for often it is his own players who block his route if they are unaware he is coming.

② Efficient defence at corners nullifies a major attacking route for the opposition. If it also obtains possession, those with the ball should look to retain it whilst the defence re-forms or release it forward in a fast counter attack.

③ Against a regular short corner tactic by opponents, the defence can put players in front *and* behind the near-post jumper.

● The Defence at Corner Kicks:
Sheffield Wednesday v. Leeds United 1992

Ⓐ In response to Sheridan's short kick to Bart-Williams, Sterland moves from his near

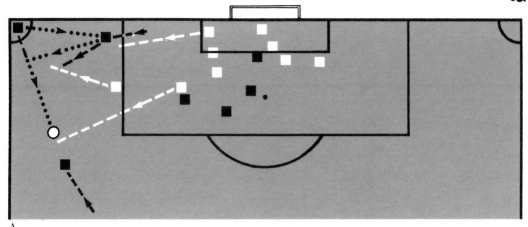

A

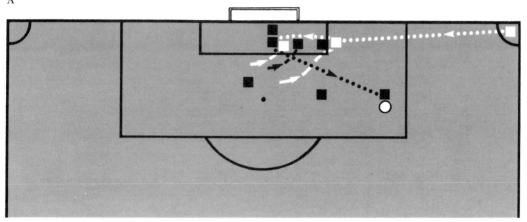

B

■ Sheffield Wednesday
□ Leeds United

post position to make the return ball to Sheridan the logical pass. Meanwhile, Wallace has moved to check any run or cross by Sheridan and the two Wednesday players are held man-to-man. Sheridan's only way out is a back pass to King, his full-back, but the pass is partially blocked by Wallace and

Shutt is able to intercept before the ball reaches King.

Ⓑ To a Leeds right-wing corner, the Sheffield defenders move to cover Whyte's run to the near post and, though the Leeds defender does get his head to the cross and flicks it on across goal, there are sufficient numbers available to head the ball clear. The corner to the near post is very common now and a defence must cover both the front jumper and those likely to feed off any glanced header.

The Offside Trap

● The Tactic

Abused and overused, the offside trap is a legitimate tactic of the game but not a contributor to the artistry of a fast moving match. The law has been amended and will surely be changed again but, for the present, it remains a major element of the defensive armoury of any senior team.

It is a tactic which needs co-ordination. A single defender, if he knows himself to be the nearest of his team to their goal, or more likely the back line of the defence must judge when to hold his position or move forward together so as to put an opponent offside. Attacks are immediately nullified, the opponents' spirit dulled, and the opportunity to start an attack from the fresh possession gained from the resultant kick.

● Learning the Tactic

① Many tactics can be learnt or refined in a match situation. If a defence is deliberately to employ the offside trap it must practise it in training until the signal can be acted upon without hesitation.

② The goalkeeper must play his part in a team using this tactic. He can be ready to cover an attacker who 'beats' the trap, call for it to be used more or less often, and alert his team-mates to the means the opposition are using to break it.

③ Level is on-side. The attacker no longer has to be *behind* the last defender.

● The Tactic in Use

① In all but the professional leagues there is the chance of encountering inefficient officials and a team must be ready to abandon the tactic in such circumstances.

② If the trap is beaten or offside not flagged, defenders must be ready to react by running back to cover rather than stand rooted in a vain appeal to the officials.

③ The runner from midfield, breaking through the defensive line just after the ball is played, is the biggest danger to an offside policy . . . and therefore the best solution for the attacking side.

● The Offside Trap: Leeds United v. Manchester United 1991

Ⓐ In this example it is the attackers who are at fault rather than the defence specifically using the offside trap. Giggs plays a short ball to McClair on the Manchester left and runs on and round his team-mate who is busy evading Strachan's tackle. By the time McClair is clear and able to release the ball, his young colleague has run too far forward and is unable to get back onside in time.

Ⓑ Later in the game Leeds, who often choose to play free kicks short (see p. 42), send a high cross to the right-hand side of their opponent's penalty area. The Manchester defensive line, however, has

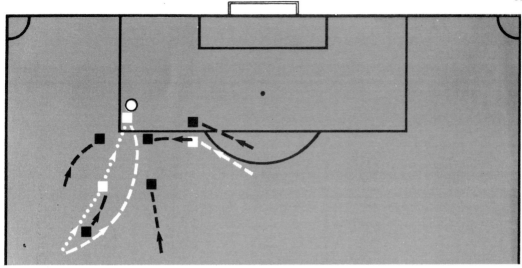

A

B

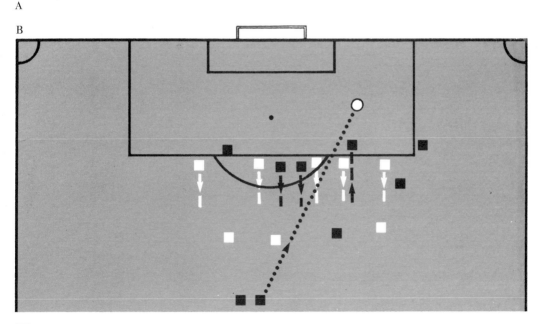

■ Leeds United
□ Manchester United

responded to a call and moves forward in unison just before the kick is taken. Though Speed probably 'beats' the trap with a clever run, both Whyte and Chapman are caught out by the defence's tactic.

▲The Leeds United teams of the early 1970s boasted a fine midfield in which Johnny Giles demonstrated great awareness and the ability to govern and change the direction of attack. (Colorsport)

▶ George Best was the master of most soccer tactics and yet retained the flair which made him special. His close control, at pace or in confined areas, was remarkable. (Colorsport)

Back Pass to the Goalkeeper

● The Tactic

Until the growing clamour for this element of the game to be outlawed is successful and whilst it is within the laws of the game, it can be used as required and is tactically valuable. Though its negative use for time wasting purposes is not to be encouraged, the keeper is a 'paid up' member of the team and should be used as such when the need arises and it is safe to do so.

Defenders will too often take the option of the pass back when more constructive possessional moves can be made – this is just as likely to produce an error because such a pass is often made in panic – but in dangerous situations the properly executed pass to the goalkeeper can promptly avert danger. It should be played when alternative moves are risky and when defensive outfielders and the keeper are all watching for it. It is always safest when the ball stays on the ground – lofted passes are more likely to lack the necessary pace or be overhit – and is played straight at the goalkeeper. If it is impossible to pass directly at the keeper, the defender should play the ball wide of goal and risk conceding a corner rather than scoring an own goal.

● Learning the Tactic

① Defenders and their keeper should agree on the call which will be given by the keeper when the pass is safe. All players should be aware of how the ground conditions can come into play.

② As with so much training, the pass back must be practised when under pressure as will surely be the case in match situations.

③ The alternatives to passing back should be played on the training ground and the goalkeeper should become used to attackers chasing the ball passed back to him.

● The Tactic in Use

① Having completed the back pass the defender should aim to regain the preferred defensive formation as soon as possible.

② The defender, having played the ball to the keeper's hands, may then be the best choice of distribution and must be prepared for the throw out.

③ Both the defender making the pass and his team-mates should watch the ball into the keeper's hands in case a fumble causes them to move to his support.

● The Back Pass to the Goalkeeper: ⓐ Crystal Palace v. Chelsea 1991

The effect of an attack breaking down and a sudden, well-directed through ball, causes

Chelsea to be left with two defenders marking two forwards. Elliott turns to track the pass with Gabbiadini close behind; further infield Cundy marks Bright who chases goalwards hoping that his team-mate will reach the pass ahead of Elliott and cross the ball.

For Elliott a right-footed clearance to touch is difficult and a sideways pass to Cundy unwise; there is no other supporting defender close and he could be dispossessed if he seeks to bring the ball under control. His back pass to Hitchcock is hit firmly and straight, the keeper gathers it cleanly and prepares to clear. A well executed forward move by Crystal Palace has been cancelled out by efficient, safe and quick-witted defence.

A

■ Chelsea
□ Crystal Palace

● *The Back Pass to the Goalkeeper:* Ⓑ *Aston Villa v. Tottenham Hotspur 1992*

Daley breaks clear in midfield and is pursued by Stewart. As he accelerates towards the Spurs penalty area both Stewart, on his left, and van den Hauwe, on his right, close in but neither wants to risk a lunging tackle. With Daley preparing to cross or shoot, the full-back decides on the back pass so throws himself forward at the ball just ahead of Daley and pushes it back to Thorstvedt. This was an efficient defensive move which regained possession as well as preventing a throw-in, corner, cross or shot.

B

■ Tottenham Hotspur
□ Aston Villa

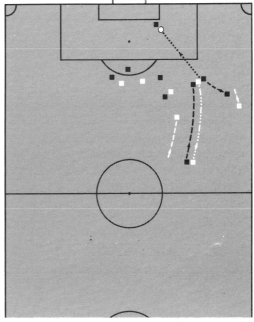

69

Goalkeeping Angles

● The Tactic

The goalkeeper defends a net with an opening of $24' \times 8'$. With him standing in the centre of his goal-line it is clear that he is protecting only the middle portion, until diving or jumping. Even in this standing position he can narrow the angle by moving forward in a line towards the ball; if, in addition, he then dives to spread his body he can be covering the whole area between his goal posts.

By narrowing the angle a keeper gives himself a better chance to save or block the eventual shot and puts a pressure on the player shooting. The danger in straying too far from the line is that the keeper leaves himself open to the lofted shot or out of position if the ball is passed laterally rather than aimed at goal.

● Learning the Tactic

① Goalkeepers must be constantly aware of their position in relation to the goal, e.g. central to the line between the middle of the goal and the ball. This can be trained for by placing a number of stationary balls at a distance from goal and having the keeper place himself to cover shots from each position without checking his net.

② Alert goalkeepers should be watching for shots being attempted and prepare to move out to narrow the angle if they notice the build up to a shot or a forward breaking through to shoot.

③ They must guard against diving too soon or advancing too early, where a shot can be lifted over them.

● The Tactic in Use

① In leaving his line to narrow the angle, the keeper leaves his line unprotected. Defenders should move to cover this gap; attackers should be aware of the unguarded net if the ball breaks free.

② The keeper will aim to save the ball cleanly and claim possession but he and his defenders must be ready to reclaim the ball if he can only parry it.

● Goalkeeping Angles

Here are some diagrams which will demonstrate how the goalkeeper can narrow the angle, creating the largest possible barrier to the opponent.

In example Ⓐ it is immediately clear how the advancing keeper blocks more of the target the closer he gets to the shooter but if he gets his line of approach wrong – and attackers seldom stand still or approach in a straight line – he may be leaving his net less well protected than if he had stayed on his line. In example Ⓑ it can be seen that the keeper may have fully covered the shot to his left but has offered an inviting gap to his right.

In diagram Ⓒ we illustrate the problem caused by a keeper diving too early at the feet of an onrushing forward. The low, thin barrier almost forces the opponent to lift the ball into the vacant area the goalie has left. By staying in a crouched position for longer, as in picture **D**, the keeper still has the option of the dive, if his reactions are fast enough, but he is also prohibiting the chip shot and, even if it is tried, is in a stance which enables him to jump to cover it.

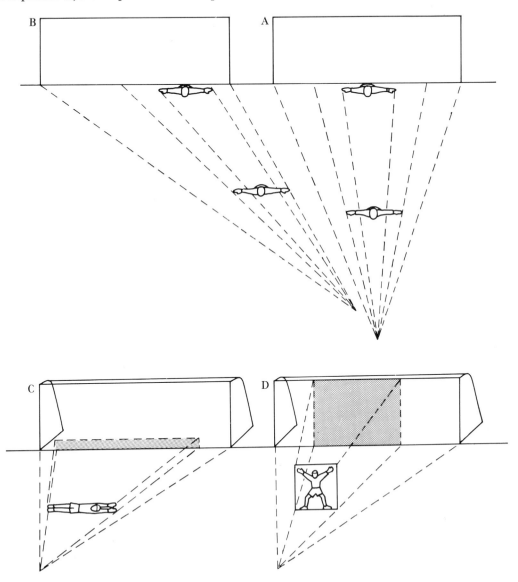

Goalkeeper Distribution

● The Tactic

As we have established earlier, clearing punts by the keeper can produce good attacking chances at the opposite end of the pitch – on occasions goals have been scored direct from them.

This method of clearance remains the most popular but a team is well advised to employ alternatives – the majority of which offer a better chance of retaining possession – so as to keep opponents guessing and open up different modes of attack.

The roll-out or short kick to a nearby defender ensures possession even if in a defensive area of the field, the overarm throw can quickly and accurately get the ball to a player in midfield and a mid-range kick will fall where there are more team-mates to challenge for it.

A keeper who distributes accurately is a major asset but his skill is, of course, nullified unless his colleagues are alert to his moves.

● Learning the Tactic

① A goalkeeper must work on the accuracy of his kicks and throw, and can do so on his own should there be no alternative.

② His clearances must allow for his players' movements, i.e. be played in front of a team-mate running forward, not to his position when the ball is cleared.

③ Outfield players should learn to make

themselves available, in space, as soon as the ball is safely in the keeper's hands.

● The Tactic in Use

① A keeper must watch how the opposition react to particular clearances and be ready to adapt if they counter one method especially well.

② It is unwise to experiment or attempt any untried clearance in a match. The receiving player may not respond as the keeper expects and induce panic in himself and others.

③ A goalie should never take his eye off his clearance! (See Something Special p. 78).

● Goalkeeping Distribution: Leeds United v. Manchester United 1992

Both keepers in this match use a variety of clearance methods; each has a long throw and a prodigious kick but can change their strategy to suit the circumstances.

Ⓐ Lukic spots McAllister in space on the left wing and quickly overarms his throw to the feet of the midfielder whilst some Manchester players are claiming a free kick. McAllister has time to control the ball and move forward without challenge before passing to Speed who then allows Hodge to take over and drive in a diagonal cross.

Ⓑ The Leeds keeper is one of those who

have followed the new trend of rolling the ball outside their area, once the players have retreated to midfield, and then clearing the ball from the ground rather than with a punt. Clearly, he and others using this tactic feel they can achieve more accuracy and, certainly, length. In this example he reaches the edge of his opponents' area where they struggle to defend the attack.

© (Not illustrated) In the other goal, Scmeichel normally prefers to punt but later in this game he jumps up from a diving save to throw an enormous overarm clearance from near his own penalty spot to a point five yards outside the Leeds area where Hughes is fouled in his attempt to reach the ball. The pace and low trajectory of such a clearance present fresh problems for a defence.

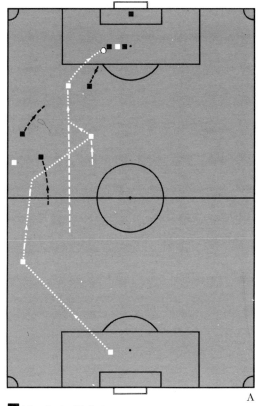

A

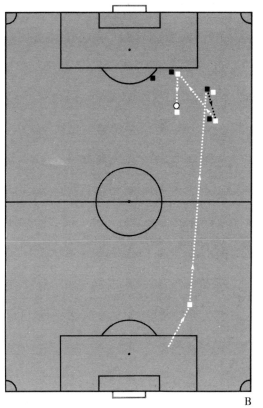

B

■ Manchester United
☐ Leeds United

Tackling

● The Tactic

The tackle is such a fundamental part of the game of soccer that it might surprise the reader to see it presented as a tactic. The truth is, however, that the tactics employed in deciding when to make a tackle, getting in the position to make it, and covering those who are making the challenge are not only worthy of study but can be improved to bring more success.

The first requirement of a defender is to delay the opposition, then induce an error or make a tackle, and regain possession. A rash tackle can concede a free kick, a weak or poorly-timed one is unlikely to win the ball, to delay in making a tackle or missing the opportunity to make one keeps the ball advancing on your goal.

The tactical element in tackling, therefore, is when, how and where to tackle, ensure the tackle or the ricochet from it wins possession, and cover the man making the challenge. Strong, successful tactics can destroy the opponents spirit.

● Learning the Tactic

① All players will be required to tackle so all should learn the skill. The correct position from which to make a tackle is in front or alongside the player with the ball so train to get to the best point for tackling.

② Keeping the eye on the ball – the primary need of all ball games – is critical in tackling.

③ In tackling the law endorses the player's aim – to win the ball – so always put your foot to the ball. Dispossessing an opponent has nothing to do with his feet, ankles or shins, only the ball he is using.

● The Tactic in Use

① All but the very best players are stronger with one foot than the other. Defenders will try to force an attacker to run to their weakest side where they find control and distribution more difficult and are more susceptible to the tackle. This, of course, applies in the reverse.

② The tackle will often leave the defender on the ground and momentarily out of the game. His team-mates must counter for this; opponents will seek to use it to their advantage.

● Tackling: Nottingham Forest v. Arsenal 1991

Anyone who doubts that tackling can be tactical need only watch a world class defender in action. In this game, England international Des Walker displays all the intelligence, timing, bravery and speed required to reach his standard of play. He adopts specific tactics for various Arsenal forwards, makes a remarkable series of interventions and clearances throughout the game and is instrumental in his team's victory.

We show five tackles made by Walker. Each one required a different skill and tactical thought.

Ⓐ Merson breaks clear at pace on the right. Walker, knowing he must delay or tackle the Arsenal player, waits until his opponent pushes the ball a foot or so too far in front of him. His lightning strike knocks the ball into touch.

Ⓑ A sharp forward ball from Rocastle reaches Smith, with Walker close behind him. The defender knows of Smith's ability to shield the ball and turn defenders so his tackle is quick and direct the moment the ball arrives.

■ Nottingham Forest
□ Arsenal

Ⓒ As Campbell receives a through ball, Smith makes a fine run in support, giving his young partner the chance of a quick pass into his path. This would take Walker, marking Campbell, out of the game and cause real danger, so the defender launches himself at the arriving ball to reach it before Campbell and stop the threat.

Ⓓ Again, Merson's pace sees him dashing into the Forest area between Walker and Pearce. Walker's sliding tackle is perfectly timed, all-embracing and fair.

Ⓔ A delightful head-on by Smith puts Campbell clear in the penalty area. From a stride behind the young Arsenal striker, Walker turns, gets alongside and stretches to the bouncing ball to knock it away for a corner.

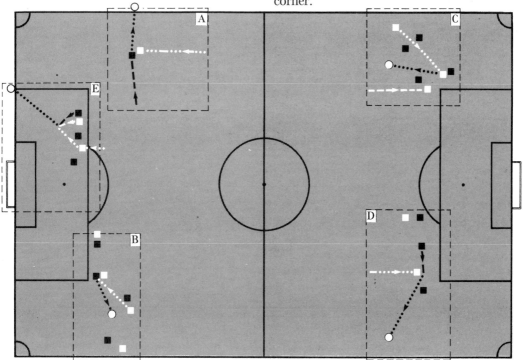

75

The Keeper as a Defender

● The Tactic

The modern goalkeeper should always be ready to assume the role of a final line of outfield defence. In the event of an attacker breaking clear or of the ball being played into space behind the last defender, it may not be safe for him to allow the ball to run into the penalty area or to rely on his defenders getting back to collect the ball. In these circumstances the keeper must clear the ball to safety by kicking it to touch or far enough upfield to enable him and his defence to re-form.

Judgement on the part of the keeper is all-important, as is a good understanding with his defence. A keeper who is constantly roaming the edge of his area like a caged animal, eager to dash anywhere to what he perceives to be a danger point, can be a handicap; a goalie who efficiently anticipates the need to rush from goal to clear in this manner can be a real benefit to a defensive line, knowing that there is a 'defender' behind them.

● Learning the Tactic

① The elementary lesson of watching the ball is crucial here as the keeper needs to assess the pace and direction of a through ball or a breaking attacker, not just notice that the defence has been breached.

② By leaving his goal area the keeper is susceptible to the lob and he must be sure that he has a good chance of achieving a clearance before he makes his move; if in doubt, he should hold back as this still leaves him with a chance to defend.

③ Though this is a play introduced as a panic solution to danger, it must still be practised on the training ground.

● The Tactic in Use

① The preferred clearance is into touch; it helps if the keeper can kick with both feet.

② If the keeper gets a good contact and moves the ball back upfield, the resulting change of direction can be turned to his team's advantage.

③ If the attempted clearance remains in play, in the possession of the attacking team, and the goalkeeper is out of position, defenders must concentrate on reaching the goal line to protect the net.

● The Keeper as a Defender: Tottenham Hotspur v. F C Porto 1991

Kostadinov makes a quick strike from the halfway line and exchanges passes with Timofte which send him clear of the square defensive line of the London team. Thorstvedt will be allowing the Porto player a free left-wing cross from a dangerous position if he fails to make a challenge but the Spaniard's line is taking him perilously close to the edge of the penalty area and the keeper cannot risk trying to claim the ball with his hands.

■ Tottenham Hotspur
□ F.C. Porto

As the Spurs outfield defenders race back in support, Thorstvedt runs to make a sliding tackle on Kostadinov. With timing his team-mates would be proud of, he tackles just as the player pushes the ball forward again and thus is able to knock the ball to the sidelines and safety. The Spurs defence would have had three players back in the goal area should the keeper have failed to clear.

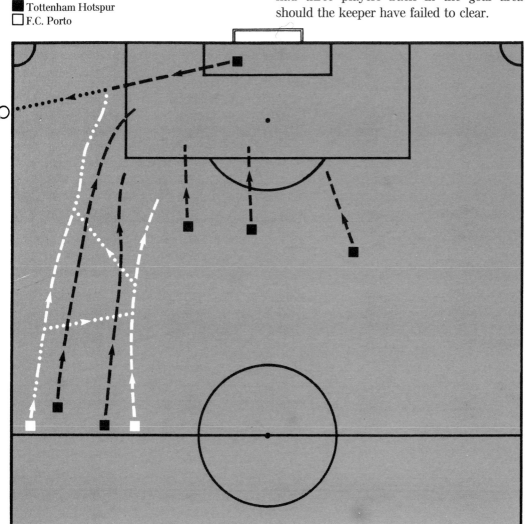

Something Special

Perhaps you cannot coach the ability to suddenly produce something special in the midst of a match, something which takes the breath away in the participants, spectators . . . and the person performing the skill. It is still a part of the senior game which draws the crowds and is more likely to be demonstrated by a player who has complete concentration, strong basic skills and, perhaps above all, the daring to try *something special*.

Here are some wonderful examples:

Ⓐ The Volley: Fulham v. Leicester 1974

In this FA Cup match a cross from the left reaches Alan Mullery at knee height. Rather than try to control the ball, he hits it on the volley with astonishing power and accuracy, and with such immediacy that spectators were unsure what was happening. The young Peter Shilton deserved credit for attempting to save a ball which few keepers would have seen.

Ⓑ The Clearance Returned: West Ham United v. Manchester City 1970

Corrigan, the City keeper, receives a back pass at his right-hand edge of the penalty area. He punts clear and makes back to his goal-line. The kick, however, is a weak one and falls to Ronnie Boyce still inside the Manchester half. As the ball reaches him, Boyce, realising Corrigan has not yet got back to his goal area, hammers a volley fully 40 yards directly into the unguarded net.

Ⓒ The 'Donkey Kick' Free Kick: Coventry v. Everton 1970

Willie Carr, Ernie Hunt and other Coventry team-mates stand over the ball at a free kick 20 yards from goal. Between them and the line is a substantial Everton 'wall'. Carr grips the stationary ball between his heels, jumps – kicking his heels behind him and sending the ball into the air – and then watches with delight as Hunt drives what is now a volley, over the wall and into the net.

Ⓓ The Dream Shot: Hereford United v. Newcastle United 1972

Every season sees a clutch of 'dream' goals where shots from distance fly unerringly into the roof of the net. This classic helped Hereford, then a non-League team, to Cup victory over mighty Newcastle. Radford plays a one-two and scores from 30 yards; spectacular indeed but he had the nerve to attempt the shot, the power to strike from distance and the skill to keep the ball down.

Ⓔ The Long Chip Shot: Liverpool v. Everton 1977

As discussed earlier, the chip shot is a wonderful spectacle when successful. Keegan, at the left corner of the penalty area, lays the ball square to McDermott who cleverly avoids one rash challenge, looks up and, seeing the keeper outside the six-yard box, drifts an inch-perfect chip over him and into the net. A moment of coolness in the heat of a Merseyside derby!

ⓕ *Close Control: Manchester United v. Southampton 1971*

By definition, intricate close control is a personal skill which is used on the spur of the moment; practice makes perfect and natural flair does not hurt either. In this example Charlton drills a low diagonal ball into the penalty area. McIlroy allows the ball to run to Best near the penalty spot. Two defenders immediately lunge forward; the first is beaten by the ball being dragged backward, the second by a deft flick to the right. In a moment the ball is curled wide of the advancing keeper and the crowd shrieks with delight.

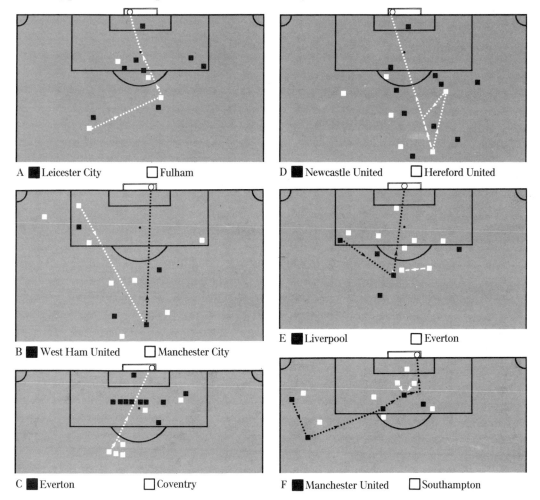

A ■ Leicester City □ Fulham

B ■ West Ham United □ Manchester City

C ■ Everton □ Coventry

D ■ Newcastle United □ Hereford United

E ■ Liverpool □ Everton

F ■ Manchester United □ Southampton

Index